The Lost Mind of Buffalo Morgan

Sick & Funny Comedy from Buffalo's Vegas Show.

I0231314

By: Barry Hemmerle

Edited By: Amy Lignor

Copyright © 2012 Freedom of Speech Publishing, Inc.

All rights reserved.

ISBN: 1938634217
ISBN-13: 978-1-938634-21-5

DEDICATION

This book is dedicated to my fans. I'd be just another guy giggling at the voices in my head with you. So thank you.

Barry Hemmerle

The Lost Mind of Buffalo Morgan
Sick & Funny Comedy from Buffalo's Vegas Show
By Barry Hemmerle

2012 copyright by Freedom of Speech Publishing, Inc.

All rights reserved. No part of this book may be reproduced, distributed,
or transmitted in any form or by any means, without permission in
writing from the publisher.

Printed in the United States of America
The publisher offers discounts on this book when ordered in bulk quantities. For more information, contact Sales Department, Phone 815-290-9605, Email: sales@FreedomOfSpeechPublishing.com

Product and company names mentioned herein are the trademarks or registered trademarks of their respective owners.

Freedom of Speech Publishing, Leawood KS, 66224
www.FreedomOfSpeechPublishing.com

ISBN: 1938634217
ISBN-13: 978-1-938634-21-5

A SPECIAL THANK YOU TO YOU!

On behalf of everyone at Freedom Of Speech Publishing, thank you for choosing The Lost Mind of Buffalo Morgan: Sick & Funny Comedy from Buffalo's Vegas Show for your reading enjoyment.

As an added bonus and special thank you, for purchasing choosing The Lost Mind of Buffalo Morgan: Sick & Funny Comedy from Buffalo's Vegas Show, you can enjoy discounts and special promotions on other Freedom of Speech Publishing products. Visit www.freedomeofspeech.com/vip to learn more.

We are committed to providing you with the highest level of customer satisfaction possible. If for any reason you have questions or comments, we are delighted to hear from you. Email us at: cs@freedomofspeechpublishing.com or visit our website at http://freedomofspeechpublishing.com/contact-us-2/. If you enjoyed The Lost Mind of Buffalo Morgan: Sick & Funny Comedy from Buffalo's Vegas Show, visit www.freedomofspeechpublishing.com for a list of similar books or upcoming books.

Again, thank you for your patronage. We look forward to providing you more entertainment in the future.

Barry Hemmerle

CONTENTS

	Acknowledgments	vii
	Introduction	1
1	Who the Hell is Buffalo Morgan?	4
2	These People Did this for Me	28
3	Sex - A – The Good	44
4	Sex - B – The Bad	57
5	Sex – C – The Ugly	67
6	The Echo – Till Death Do We Part Part Part	78
7	L.L.A. – Life's Little Anasthesias	100
8	I'll Take Five Losing Lottery Tickets, Please	125
9	All I Want for Christmas is a Cannon Bolted to my Car	139
10	A Big Pile of Conglomafux	148
11	Pets – No, Really	196

ACKNOWLEDGEMENTS

I'd like to give special thanks to two people above all else.

My son, Dan, who banged it out on his computer in record time. With my keyboard skills, I wouldn't have reached my first pinga joke yet.

And to my illustrator, Eric Brown. I hope you have a long, successful career… in art.

I hope you enjoy my journey on stage. If you'd like to read more on my soulful side, I have two books of poetry available on Amazon.com. But you won't find any butterflies and unicorns in them. More like love, lust, and world domination.

And they are…

"Poems of love and Other Creepy Crawly Emotions" and, "The Book of Gemini"

Introduction

So I'm on stage, in Vegas, doing my act and this older fella is sitting up front. After every punch line, he'd say, "Huh, what was that?" and I'd repeat the punch line. After a while of this, I told him I'd write a book of my act and he can read it. He laughed and said he'd buy it. So did about a dozen people in the audience… DING.

This book came to be over an ad-lib..

Half an ad-lib. Over the next six months, I watched old videos of my ever-changing act. A lot of my classic bits that I've retired over the years have been brought back to the light in this book.

The one thing I noticed as I watched my videos is, even back then, like now, I was having the time of my life. One of the good decisions I've made in this lifetime was my career choice.

When I get up every day, I can't wait to get to work. Of course, I wake up at 2:00 in the afternoon and I have seven hours to get to work, but I love my job. Also, if you purchased one of my "Buffalo Morgan beat up your honor roll student," bumper stickers and would like me to sign it, please bring it to my next show.

And the last thing, If you've been to my show or most any comedy show, you know some of the topics can get... graphic... adult... childish adult, that'll work.

To make it "less offensive," the word "penis" will be changed to pinga. Of the hundred slang words, I chose "Pinga." It sounds Disney-like.

Also "vagina" will be changed to "scootch". When I was growing up, that's what my friends called it. Say it, it's fun... scootch.

I will be dropping the "F-bomb" in all its glory, periodically.

Other than that, nothing else is censored in this book... NOTHING.

Chapter 1
Who the Hell is Buffalo Morgan?

Just in from the Hell Hole in Las Vegas... Buffalo Morgan...

Good evening and thank you for joining me tonight. I'm sorry if I'm a little late. My G.P.S. was screwing with me again. It said I couldn't get here from there.

The last time I got quality information like that I had a wedding ring on.

So I just got in from Las Vegas. I love it out there. I just wish I knew how to gamble. It sucks paying the mortgage on a hotel I don't own.

I'm also not crazy about their slogan, "What happens in Vegas, stays in Vegas." I enjoyed the company of eight different ladies in six days, I wanna tell somebody!

As a matter of fact, there's a lot of saying I don't agree with. Like, "Money doesn't buy happiness." Like hell it don't. Hawaii makes me happy but without money I'm stuck here with you guys... no offense. New underwear makes me happy but they're not just going to let me take it. They want money. So, money does buy happiness and clean underwear.

Another one. "If a tree falls and no one is around to hear it, does it make a sound?" Duh. Do people think that because you don't see it, it won't make a sound? I hit a golf ball last year. I didn't see it but I'm pretty sure I heard it shatter a windshield. But I'll tell you I didn't make a sound as I crept away.

My favorite, "The customer is always right." Ask any waitress, teller, or store employee. Half the time, the customer is a numbskull demanding a miracle.

"I'd like a lawnmower that will cut the lawn itself."

"Yeah, well I'd like to go to Hawaii by using my dazzling smile but that's not happening either." There are a lot more but I'll just stick with those for now.

Some questions don't have a definitive answer. Some people think "middle age" is between 35 and 40. Unless you die at 40 then for you, it was 20. I don't think it's really a number; it's more of a feeling. For me, it was 42. That's when I started shaving my ears, plucking my nose hair, and my 6-pack abs became a keg. My pinga had a roof.

It got to the point that when I went clothes shopping; I actually had to try them on to see if they fit.

I don't like this aging thing. It's really throwing a lot of extra work my way. Last week I had to use a magnifying glass to see the year on an old penny. And it took me 45 minutes to find the magnifying glass. My mom said, "Well maybe you're getting senile."

I'm already thinking that so don't help me...

I never really thought about getting old until things started breaking down. Like last year I punched a stop sign.. Well, because it was there. I've been punching stop signs for 40 years, this time I fractured a finger.

And this time I didn't fix it with duct tape. I went to a doctor... a real doctor. After he set my finger, he did some tests. Later he said to me, "Your cholesterol is a little high."

"Cholesterol? What the hell is that?"

Then he started asking about my drinking. He said, "So, how much alcohol do you drink in an average week?"

I said, "Enough"

So he reaches into his pocket and hands me an A.A. card. Then I handed him an A.A.A. card. That's Alcoholics Anonymous Anonymous. That's for people that want to quit trying to stop drinking. Yeah, that's right. I'm no quitter.

So by a show of hands, how many of you waited in your doctor's office soooo long, you started going through his drawers looking for things. You know, thermometers and band aids. You know you're not going to find the "good" stuff in there. Unless your doctor's a junkie, then you're in the game.

I always hoped to hit the mother lode. "Oh my god, look at all this shit. It's... It's... It's like high school."

I don't ask for much in a doctor.. A steady hand and skinny fingers. Guys, when you get your first prostate exam, it will all become very clear to you.

I just had my second exam. I intentionally freaked out my doctor.

The first time, I jumped and squealed like a schoolgirl. You know it's coming but it's still a shock. The last time, I stood there and took it. I didn't even flinch. Then I turned around and said, "I love you too."

I'm getting it though and I really should be more careful. I don't even have health insurance. Can you believe that? Most comedians do not have health insurance. But I do have car insurance. So you know what that means right? If I start having chest pains, I have to jump in my car and hit a telephone pole before a doctor will see me.

That's a little money saving tip from me to you.

I think I'm still in good shape. I play sports, I still do wild things. I also think I'm a perfect one night stand.

Look, I can drink; I can hold an intelli... intell... a smart conversation. I know my way around a women's body pretty darn good. And in the morning, when you wake up, you'll look at me and say, "Eh, I could have done worse."

I like to think of myself as pretty intelligent. Yeah, that's right, I just looked it up. I think that for every problem, there's a solution.

Like this. In an airport, there are signs that say, "Welcome to America. Please learn the language…" What? There's not? Well that's the problem then. My solution was learning how to say in Spanish,

"Please learn to speak English, por favor."

But, let's get them signs up. When you're here for five years and you can't order a bowl of soup.. You're not trying very hard.

I went into a convenience store and ordered a hot dog and I walked out with lottery tickets. Losing lottery tickets.

I think the world is spinning just a little too fast and it's hard to keep up. From a guy's perspective, the last 10,000 years have been a huge waste of time. Back in the Stone Age, women were naked. Then we evolved, and developed the internet, so we can see women naked.

And who in the world invented the I.R.S.? I pay my taxes for the same reason you guys do... FEAR! If they can fuck up Joe Louis' life, I'd hate to think what they can do to me. I always pay extra to be sure. Even when I fill out my forms, I try to make them chuckle.

"Name?" "Buffalo Morgan." "Occupation?" "Comedian." "Describe what you do." "I manufacture and distribute probable yet incredible nuggets of sugar-coated bullshit."

"How much were you paid?"

"I was paid in beer and scootch."

I don't think our government will be happy until we're all in a constant state of multi-tasking. One hand digging a ditch while the other is flipping burgers.

Some people have a real problem with multi-tasking. It's not that hard. Just before I hit this stage, I was sitting on this toilet, smoking a joint and reading Reader's Digest.

It's not that tough.

Last week, I tried starting my own urban legends. They're not bad. The first one is Dr. Seuss was inspired to write "Green Eggs and Ham" after having breakfast at a Stuckey's. It has a gram of credibility.

The other is the president of Hertz Rent-A-Car changed his name years ago because he didn't want to the world to know his name is Dick Hertz. Again, it has a possibility.

It's all image... How you perceive something you don't know. Like me. I'm kinda successful and make a decent buck. But you don't know me when I leave the stage. Watch this, raise your hands if you think I'm going to go home to my mansion and sniff a mountain of cocaine then go bang my three playboy wives.

See, look at the hands. Now this is probably a little closer to reality. I'm going to the bar in the next room, run up a tab that would make your head spin then sneak out the backdoor.

Hey, it's a recession... and I'm un-rich.

But I do love my fans and you guys. It's great to see you here. Are any of my groupies here tonight? No, well maybe tomorrow night. Oh yeah, we have groupies. They're a little different then rock and roll groupies though.

R+R groupies are about 20 years old and comic groupies are about 50... 55. The Rock and Rollers lift their shirts to flash you their boobies. A comic groupie lowers her slacks to show you hers.

The rockers have the best come-on lines, "You wanna fuck me in the limo." The comic groupies, again, a little lame, "You wanna come back to the trailer park? I have a half a bottle of gin with your name on it." And groupies are different from place to place. Like in New York, I'm always signing women's breasts. In Vegas, I sign nipples. It's what they want. I feel like a diamond cutter, B... (lick tip of pen) U... (lick tip of pen). Two of them and I'm ready for bed.

Hey, I just remembered, I'm celebrating something tonight. The 12th light on my dashboard came on today and the car still moves. It's so exciting driving that thing. And when I'm low on gas, I have a baker's dozen.

If you're gonna be poor, this is the country to do it in. I almost don't want another car. I like my P.O.S. I even like my little bumper sticker, " I didn't get a B.A. at Rutgers but I did get a D.U.I. at Villanova."

If big money comes my way then I'm sure money will start dropping from the sky everywhere. I'll win a couple lotteries, go on "Who Wants to be a Millionaire" with Regis. That would be exciting.

"Tell us about yourself, Buffalo."

"Well Rege, I like coke. I'm married to three playboy bunnies and I have a huge pinga. I mean Sunday softball bat. By the way, ever drop the hammer on Kelly? No... is that your final answer?"

It's all about money. Everybody would like to pay their bills on time... and do that... that chewing thing a couple times a day. What's that called… oh yeah, eating. I don't know why but food is so addictive. I get cranky when it's not around. Everybody does. Even if I'm just cutting back on my food for a diet, there's a good chance someone might get hurt.

"Wanna grab a burger?"

"NO, I DON'T WANNA GRAB A BURGER." Sorry about that. Some poor people steal to eat. That's why there are cameras everywhere. I'm glad there's cameras everywhere. If some asshole caves my head in with a brick for the three dollars of change in my pocket, I want him humiliated and killed.

But I'm not a big fan of those intersection cameras. Last year, I got a ticket in the mail for 9four dollars for blowing a red light, and it comes with a crystal clear photo. My picture shows a rare double bird.

I'm thinking of making that my new promo photo. Or get a smaller copy for a business card. Folks will remember that.

Maybe sell the picture to the I.R.S. They could paint a 30 foot high picture of me as you enter their building. "Yeah, this is not going to end well."

The Lost Mind of Buffalo Morgan

Do you think there are people with their little audit papers in their hand, getting ready to walk into an I.R.S. building, knowing in their best year, they haven't earned a fraction of a percent of the money the I.R.S. says they owe after late fees and fines accrue, and say to themselves, "I think I'll have a couple beers and think about this."

Next thing you know, you're waking up in a 747 with a "How to Speak Spanish" book in your lap.

"Please buckle up, we'll be landing in Ecuador in 10 minutes."

Know what's always in season... Freedom.

I think I would run. I have two allergies... prison and anal rape. I don't like them... separately or together.

I can see myself in prison. Not for something evil but for something stupid. Like running to a convenient store and accidently parking in a worn out handicapped spot, go in, buy a snack, come out to find a cop writing me a ticket and he claims he hears me cursing him out, which was a complete fabrication.

"What are you in for?"

"A box of cookies and telling a cop to go fuck himself. You're not going to make me your bitch, are you?" I don't think I'd be very good at the whole sex/rape thing and I have a problem with my second and third lower vertebrae. I can only sleep on my back. I'd probably cry a lot. Then how much fun would I be, right?

I start hyperventilating when I'm driving and a cop gets behind me. I haven't done anything in 30 years and my urine is... pretty clean, but I know if I get pulled over, he'll find a bag of coke from the last owner or the Lindbergh baby in the trunk. I think I worry because it might be the day I say something really stupid.

"Sir, can I see your license?"

"Which one... crap."

"Do you know who fast you were going?"

"about... 87, dammit."

"Have you been drinking tonight?"

"Wait a minute. Let me think that one over."

Do you think it's an awkward conversation in court between a lawyer and a guy sentenced to a long stretch?

"Well, the judge said 50 years but with good behavior, I can see it being cut in half."

"Really, well, fuck you.. No wait, take one of my cards."

Here's one of life's great ironies. I think I'd make a great juror but I fight hard to get out of jury duty. Go figure. If I would ever get hooked on a TV show, it would have to be Pay Per View death sentences. Make sure of their guilt, though.

Turn it into a game show.

"State number 27531, you killed a family of four and raped the cat.. Ok, spin that wheel.." click click click click.. click…. click stop.

"Hey hey, your death sentence is by… guillotine. How retro."

Now that would be a deterrent. I'm not big on TV these days. Seems like the more I pay and the more channels I get, the less there is to watch.

When I was a kid…

"Yeah, tell us all about it grandpa…"

When I was a kid, we had shows that meant something. You could learn a comical lesson about real life and they would wrap it all up in 30 minutes.

I learned how to make a radio out of coconuts, Frankenstein's monster isn't going to kill me, and if I live a clean life, I can have a 3-way with a witch and a genie.

And I also reached one of life's milestones in front of the tube...

I reached puberty watching Lynda Carter as Wonder Woman. One minute, I'm an innocent child, the next, a sick animal... I mean a man.

"Wow she is pretty. What the fuck is going on in my pants?"

But that story is for later in the show.

My point being... TV is mind-numbingly wonderful... Today, I'd be brain-dead watching these shows. I want to watch actors, not people.

"Let's see what's on today. Wow, a guy driving a truck, let's see what's going to happen... nothing... nothing... nothing... Wait, someone just called him a jerk off over his C.B. but they bleeped it. I think he said, "Fuck you." Yeah, I'm pretty sure that's what he said.

"Oh boy, let's check in on the "Kardashians" today... ok, Khloe burnt her toast... so now they're shopping for a new Mercedes. Pass."

Oh, "America's got Talent." Does that have a snake tongue English judge degrading the contestants too? We had the "Gong Show." If you sucked, you got gonged and if you wouldn't stop performing, the judges would throw bananas at you. Here, you get some twit saying, "Well darling, you're not my cup of tea. Matter of fact, you're nobodies cup of tea.. You were bloody awful." What a pinga!

And F.Y.I., back then, we had a guy on a unicycle juggling chainsaws. You have someone dancing the tango to mombo music.

But seriously, I'm glad there are outlets for future artists. Can you imagine the next generation of TV without them... "For the next ten hours, we are going to watch how many squirrels run up and down this tree." You think maybe I ought to patent that idea?

And I don't think "Survivor" is a show about surviving.

"And if Phil eats this concoction of ground up goat testicles and pineapple then he cannot be voted off the island this week."

I get it but I don't get it.

I like my version better. Put a thousand hidden motion detector cameras on a real island. Twenty contestants and a host that's on for ten seconds.

"Ok people. Here's a gun, a knife, and we buried a bag of Twizzlers on the north beach. Good luck, assholes." Then he leaves. I'd rather watch commercials.

"Are you stressed, bored, or not hungry? Call me and I'll send you a free sample baggie today... Pot... it's what's for dinner."

Chapter 2
These People Did This To Me

I'll bet your thinking I come from a very special gene pool.

That is being kind. My family was fine. It was the relatives. Nuts, all of them. With them, if you're not an alcoholic, it's because you haven't graduated from drugs yet. The penal system knows the Morgan family very well. When I was a kid, we had our own wing.

But it's not because they're criminals, just not too bright.

Stupid shit like too many jaywalking violations, forgetting to put your pants on, and of course, public drunkenness which also contributed to the first two.

My parents were Ozzie and Harriet compared to them. As a kid, I was always taken to the family reunions. I used to get the same inner feelings when I went to the zoo. You're not sure which direction to go but you want to see it all. Then, one day, I had a thought, "I'm related to these people. What if I go to sleep one night and wake up all fucked up like these folks are?" I don't think I slept for a week. I kept checking myself for warts and extra limbs.

Or I'd watch myself in the mirror for hours to see if I was going insane. That's in the chromosomes too.

My mom and dad were great. A little on the procrastinators side but ok as far as parents go. I think the worst thing they did was wait to have me circumcised.

How long?? Wanna see the bandage? I'll show you later. That's just the kind of stupid thing I'd get busted for… again.

But I grew up happy. We were poor but happy. We only had one board game growing up…

Monopoly. Remember that one? For the first two hours, you cheat to win and the next two days, you cheat to lose.

"But I wanna go to sleep, I have school tomorrow."

"Shut up and roll the dice."

They weren't perfect but they were alright.

My mom did have a strange medical condition. She went through menopause for 37 years. Which was alright because, like I said, we were poor and in the winter time, we couldn't afford heat, so anytime mom had a hot flash, we'd all gather around her.

And every night mom would read us some happy little fairy tale.

Like Hansel and Gretel being eaten by a witch... or Little Red Riding Hood being eaten by a wolf. Yeah, I know. I think mom was ad-libbing, and every time Jack and Jill would mash themselves up, mom would giggle.

I remember the first time my mom said, "Fuck you" to me. It was after one of her inspirational stories. Then she said, "Goodnight, sleep tight, don't let the bed bugs bite."

I said, "Well, if you'd clean the sheets every now and then."

That's not dysfunctional, is it?

But we're all getting older now. It's funny, she has to put on her driving glasses to find her reading glasses. She must have had the wrong glasses on yesterday. We went to the mall to watch other middle-aged people walking their parents. No, I'm kidding. I needed a shirt.

So we pass by a young girl with letters on her shirt, and my mom leans towards me and says, "That girl's shirt says she's a biotech."

I didn't have the heart to tell her it said "Bi-otch."

On the other hand, my dad was a good man. Always helping me get through life with advice.

"Hey Buff, these are the three biggest lies you'll ever hear; The check is in the mail, you won't feel a thing, and I'm from the government and I'm here to help you."

He used to say, "All the best malls have a bar in them." How true.

He loved the outdoors. When I was 14, he took me out hunting with him. My first shot, I got a rabbit. Then I picked it up, put it in the car, and we took it to the vet. Hunting isn't my thing.

And I'm just as good of a fisherman... or as I call it, "Deep Sea Barfing." My dad would make me eat a hoagie so five minutes later, I'd be chumming the water.

You know, I might need some counseling.

Come to think of it, they were always asking about work.

"When are you getting a job? When are you getting a job?"

"I don't know. I figured I'd graduate from elementary school and then check my options. Let me reach puberty before you bust my balls."

My dad did teach me how to drive. He'd toss me the keys, wash a couple valium down with a tumbler of scotch and we were on our way.

It was like taking directions from a narcoleptic. "Stop at the stop sign." Then snoring sounds. "Make a left at the light." More snoring.

But we all got along except me and my brother would fight over anything stupid. "His slice of pizza is bigger than mine." Important stuff like that.

My parents were clueless because we were so petty. "His quarter's older than mine."

"But that means your quarter is newer."

"Haha, my quarter is newer, haha."

I think a couple good backhands and our house would have been a Utopia.

One fight me and my brother had was so bad, we put a line down the middle of the bed... in indelible ink.

If it was good enough for Herman Munster and Grandpa, it was good enough for us.

One time, I bet him a nickel I could drink a Slurpee faster than him. I let him win. It was worth a nickel to watch him suffer through a brain freeze. A good lesson for later in life.

See? A shallow gene pool.

And we were considered the "normal family." We have all kinds in our family. We have southern family so rednecky their necks are purple. As kids, they played tag... with a sawed off shotgun. They took some of the gun powder out of the shells, but you still knew when you were "it." Your welts covered your ass at night.

And one of the "bestiality" brothers, (just a rumor) burned his house down as a kid. Well, his meth lab exploded... and he only had a meth lab to cover up the smell of his stills. Lots of stills.

His brother almost burned the house down a couple years earlier. Now he was the real scientist of the family. He cut the cord of a table lamp and exposed the wires. Then he put the wires under the rug and plugged it in. He was trying to make a flying carpet but got a nylon inferno. Twelve years later, you can still smell it. Maybe they should throw it out.

And one of my niece's conceived and gave birth in the same car.

The only dentist my aunt knows is on a soap opera.

Let me get back to that rumor about the "bestiality brothers." It was all just stories, who knows if they're true… BUT, I do go over to their house when I'm in town. And they have three dogs… bloodhounds… duh. And these dogs just lay around the house until the brothers grab that first beer of the day. The dogs would get up and fly through the screen door. They would come home the next day, so who knows?

I forget if it was Billy or Bob but one of them has a tattoo on his knuckles that says, "Incest is best." And yes, he does have twelve fingers.

He's married and he really believes it's not cheating if you do it with a relative. He's also the one that gets drunk and looks for U.F.O.'s. He said the only way he'll die happy is if he "gets an anal probe from one of those little fellas."

If there was any "animal loving" going on, it was him. He's got the kind of sense of humor to sing "Old Macdonald had a cow" while banging Old MacDonald's cow.

My Uncle Roy, their father, used to throw great parties when I was a kid. Whenever we'd show up, he'd say the same thing, "You kids stay outside. Here... Here's a case of beer to play with."

Seven was such an innocent age.

I learned my first dirty jokes from Uncle Roy. At night, us kids would be camped out in one room and Uncle Roy would come staggering in.

"Hey hey, you kids wanna hear a joke... I forgot it.. No, wait, there it is. Why did the farmer cross the road? ... say why."

"Why?"

"Because his pinga was stuck in the chicken."

"I got another, got another. What do you get when you cross an elephant with a rabbit? ... a dead rabbit with a giant asshole."

Are you seeing the same pattern with these folks as I'm seeing? And he would keep going until another adult took him somewhere else. "Why did the blonde trade her car for a convertible?... She needed more leg room."

He's the reason I got into comedy. I meant to get away from these people.

Oh yeah... New Year's Eve 1971.

Big party at Uncle Roy's and he learned a magic trick. Just before midnight, he staggers into the kids room, "Ok, you little fuckers want to see a trick?" and he holds up a giant glass of wine.

"I'm gonna turn this glass of red wine into a glass of white wine."

In two swallows, the wine is completely gone. Then he unzips his pants, pulls out his pinga, and pees into the glass. He puts it down on the table and says, "TaDa."

He proceeded to walk into the door he forgot to open. Then he mumbles, "Fuck" and he leaves.

So there's like seven of us kids between the ages of eight and 11 just sitting there, looking at each other with our mouths hanging open and before any of us can say anything, my Aunt Helen, Roy's wife, came into the room.

"There's my wine." And she grabbed the glass and started guzzling it.

And none of us kids said a word because that's how shallow our gene pool is.

One final word for this side of the family. They all work together in the same factory doing an ultimate redneck job. They make fireworks.

Now the other side of the family is much more private. A lot of them are closet alcoholics. I mean they will go into another room and do a couple shots and come back like you wouldn't notice. In the middle of a sentence, my Aunt Betty just left and came back and finished her story, reeking of scotch. No, not scootch. That's another aunt.

Aunt Betty was the worst at two things, cooking and her make-up. One year, she invited us over for Thanksgiving. She must have started drinking the week before. Her hair was matted on one side. Her lipstick went an inch past her lips and only one eyelid was done.. Sparkly blue. She looked like a hooker after Mardi Gras.

That was the year we had two dinners. The first one was turkey jerky with the bag shrink wrapped around it and a side of, "I forgot to cook the potatoes."

Dinner two was much better. Thank God for Burger King.

My other aunt, Aunt Jamie smokes three packs a day. And a lot of times, she'll accidently light the filter end but she doesn't drink. She says she can't stand the smell of alcohol. Apparently, she likes the smell of cocaine though.

I might be the only one to notice that she was going to the bathroom every ten minutes. She was wacky. She would tell you a complete five minute story in one long sentence and every so often a little white rock would tumble out of her nose.

Shallow, Shallow pool.

Talking about them makes me feel better about myself.

Did I mention it was like going to the zoo?

Chapter 3
Sex – A – The Good

The world does not spin on love.. Or hate. And no matter how much Dunkin Donuts wants you to believe it, it doesn't run on their coffee. The world runs on Jelly.. KY Jelly.

If you glue a coffee mug to a baseball bat and let a silicone goddess hold it, the men of the world will beat your door down to have it. How do you think they sold Yugo's 30 years ago??? Hot chicks.

Beer's another one. Some beers even put pictures of girls on the bottle, like St. Pauli Girl. Unlike women, a guy's look does not improve the more he drinks. And there is nothing more pathetic then a guy who's been shot down all night licking his bottle of beer.

Men and women like sex just as much but thank God women close the gate every now and then. I think most guys would have sex with any woman pretty much any time the thought came to them. If men could do anything to any woman anytime and every woman did the same, we'd still be living in mud huts, bartering a live chicken for three handfuls of tobacco and a potato.

Sex is fun, I admit it. I love sex. BUT, there are other things in life. I do not live for my pinga. He works when I tell him to work.

I've met some guys that are so caught up in sex, they're like idiots.

And you know how I hate idiots.

And I meet a lot of them.

One guy told me after my show, he's been happily married twelve years and he has two girls on the side. Then he asked me what I thought of that, and I said, "Well, the world needs pieces of shit too." A four minute friendship, a new record!

Another guy told me he named his pinga. Can you believe it? In a deep voice, he said, "I call it Chevy."... Cause it's like a rock."

I said, "Oh, I thought because it stalls and leaks fluids."

(No offense, I like Chevy's)

Come on, really. I don't care.

Guys think that because I talk about wild sex in my act, that I want to hear about their crazy shit. I don't. If I talk about a threesome, don't tell me about your foursomes, fivesomes, or sixsomes. Most of the guys telling me these stories don't look like they could masturbate without fucking it up.

If you want fantasy sex, you need looks, money, or fame... if you're a guy. Women, most women can have it any way they want. They just can't be picky. The only way most guys are having more than one woman in the room is if he's banging his girl while the maid is cleaning.

Guys get it when they can. Look at me, I'm not much to look at but I've met women and had sex with them all on the same barstool. It's all confidence. And like I said before, if everybody is having sex then nobody is inventing or picking up the trash.

I've talked to a lot of women over the years and more than half said that they've had men that knew nothing. Some couldn't figure out how to put it in. They also can't believe men are obsessed with boobs. Three or four squeezes and they're done.

The best sex advice I ever got was from my grandfather and he was getting laid in Model T's so he knows. He told me, " Buff, a woman is like a pinball machine. A gentle touch is the best touch... until you get the multi-ball, then you bang her through the wall." What a smart codger...

I remember the sex talk my dad gave me. "For God's sake, don't knock anybody up. I thought you were collecting baseball cards."

"Well, now I'm multi-tasking."

It's almost like that generation was ashamed to tell you how much fun they were having.

As a kid, I sat by my parents' bedroom door one night. I heard a lot of moaning and groaning, I thought they were paying the electric bill. Turns out they were making me a brother.

That all became clear after I started having sex. I started thinking,

"Where have I heard these noises before... Yikes... Yuck. My parents still had sex after I was born, gross."

Since you guys have been so nice tonight, I'm going to tell you a deep, dark secret about my sex life. .. No, no animals are involved. That's later. OK, the first time I had sex... with a woman... in a room... was really the second time. I guess I have to explain that, don't I? The best way I can explain it is by the time I got the condom on, it was time to take it off. I was so excited, it flew off by itself... and hit the ceiling.

I was terrible., but she was a good sport about it. She said she'd let me try it again as soon as I was ready. I looked down and said, "Ready."

Man, I loved being 14.

Once I figured out where it was supposed to go, I lasted a lot longer than the first time. But I still think I broke the two minute coitus. Then I made things worse. Out of force of habit from masturbating, I screamed out my own name. That's where I got my nickname from, "Four Stroke Morgan."

See how honest I am with you guys? Everybody else in the world thinks it has something to do with golf.

Needless to say, my girlfriend dumped me… Oh stop, you don't care and that was 35 years ago. I think I'm over her by now. At the time, I was more upset that I'd never find someone else to have sex with. My prime was ten horrific minutes. Now it was back to the "old ways"… and baseball cards.

The next day, I went out to look for a shiny new one. Girlfriend, that is, and now I had something to show on the sexual resume. I had sex once... no twice... ahhhh one and a half times.

And I did get better at it. I don't think I could have gotten worse.

One quick note about the girl that "broke my heart"... stop it. I met her at a party 10 years later. And she's talking to about a dozen people about riding a mechanical bull. Remember when that was popular? So as I walk by, I hear her whiny little voice say, "Oh, I tried it and I didn't like it."

I stopped walking just long enough to say, "Well, maybe you should try riding on top of the bull." I could hear them laughing even in the next room. Morale- If you have a chance for revenge, go for it.

I think men have more problems with pingas then women. They worry about the size, the shape. Now they even call it their "junk." I don't get it. The only guys that should be calling it their "junk" are old men that need a pill to jumpstart it. Go back to calling it "Chevy."

And guys always seem to worry about their size. I was in a bathroom today, standing at a urinal, and yes, I was peeing. There was a urinal next to me, but when someone else came in, he peed in a toilet. He looked at me and walked to a toilet. I'm not judging your pinga dude, and don't judge mine. If I'm not jabbing you in the back in the middle of the night with it, why do you care? But men do.

I was going to hold off on this next story because it falls under the drug and alcohol part of my show, but since I see some of you beginning to get comfortable with yourselves, I might as well keep the party going.

The only time I was ever concerned about my "size" was in a dream I had when I was about 20 years old. And it wasn't even one of those Sigmund Freud dreams like driving your car into a tunnel and you're really thinking about screwing your family pet. This was a real dream... kind of.

I picked up some acid for a party the next day. Yeah, L.S.D. I peed in my gene pool just as much as my relatives and I had a terrible motto pertaining to drugs back then. "If it's in my hand, then it's in my system." Once I bought the drugs, I had another motto,

"Let's just check this shit out."

So I did two pieces of it, (a couple hits.) That's street talk. Half hour goes by, an hour. An hour and 20 minutes... nothing. I go to bed.

So I wake up... in my dream, with a two foot pinga. It's like a Louisville Slugger and it had a brain so I taught it to talk. Just little parrot-like phrases like, "Sup bitch." So in this one night of dreaming, we lived a week. We went to the mall, to the pool. We were buddies... until he started to think. Then one day, he remembered this ugly bitch... I mean, this visually unappealing female I was screwing.

So in the middle of the night, he tried to bludgeon me to death. And the last thing I heard was, "Sup bitch. Sup bitch."

That was some good acid.

Where was I? Oh yeah, I love sex. Nice and simple. I have sex then I move on. No bells and whistles.. Sim.. ple. A good friend of mine is a doctor and do you know how he spends his nights when it's a full moon??? Pulling bells and whistles out of men's asses... and light bulbs and tools and food and even the occasional small rodent.

I don't get the obsession. My pinga isn't even my favorite organ. It's way down on my list... at least third. My favorite organ is my bladder. He can hold three 6-packs and still let me shoot a good game of pool. I just love good old-fashioned hetero sex.

I'm not going to say a bunch of stuff about the gay community. I have lots of gay friends and they are the nicest people... to me anyway. Doesn't it bug you when people say, "It's an abomination to God." Yeah, so is war and poverty, hypocrite. Come into the 21st century and mind your own business. Here, here's my soap box. Let's see if you can turn it into a burning cross.

A gay man kissed me after a show one time. I said, "Huh, so that's what pinga tastes like. Sorry, not my thing." Then I went home and washed my mouth out with scootch. (That's right, not scotch.)

There is one gay joke I really like… how do you know when you're in a gay church??? Only half the congregation is kneeling.

It's a classic.

Chapter 4
Sex – B – The Bad

I've comprised a small list of sex acts that I feel have nothing to do with love or lust. So to be kind, we'll call this category… twisted behavior.

This will include having sex with livestock, dead stock, plants – live or artificial, fruits and vegetables, wet sand on the beach, drilling holes in drywall and any place a pinga ends up but shouldn't.

If you have to go to the bathroom, this may be a good time.

These are real stories I've read about, seen on the news or heard from reliable sources in the south. Funny thing is, it's always guys. Women have toys and a closed door and guys get caught in the great outdoors.

Let's begin with the family pet... and technology. Man's best friend. A man suspected one of his kids was getting into his bottle of whiskey so he put a motion sensor camera in the room pointed at the bottle. The next day he checked the camera and saw his 14 year old son filling a glass up, taking a few sips, then dipping his pinga in the glass and letting Lassie lick it off. Now how bad does your acne need to be to think this is a good idea? The dad ended up getting rid of the dog... I'd have ditched the kid. "Something wrong with that boy."

Or how about the farmer that got caught screwing one of his cows by his wife. And she said she wouldn't have come into the barn except he was whistling a tune. Hold on, let me guess... Old Macdonald. That's a popular song with cow molesters.

She ended up getting half of the 23 million dollar farm.

And how do you think the cow feels, just chewing its oats, minding its own business. "Gonna be a beautiful... hey, what the hell is going on back there? Oh nice, this is the thanks I get for all the milk I give you.

Well, FYI, shorty... wrong hole. Hope you don't mind your junk smelling like methane for the next six months."

Yeah, even cows are digging the new slang.

I've always considered myself a people's person, that's one of the reasons why I got into this business. But little by little, I find myself not wanting to visit certain areas of this great country. An area I recently put on this list is Jobac, Alabama.

In Jobac, one of its citizens likes to season deer meat from the inside… OK, I'll explain.

Hunter A set up a motion detector and camera on an old deer trail; apparently to see if there's still wildlife there… and there is…

Hunter B killed a deer near the camera and not knowing the camera was there decided to "marinade" it before strapping it to the hood of his truck.

Hunter A was shocked by the footage but probably made a few bucks by selling it. I've seen it. It's grainy, it's distorted, but unless he was doing the Heimlich maneuver… he was screwing a dead deer.

Now my question, like I have one. My question is, how ugly do you have to be that you couldn't screw a live deer?

Couldn't some skank from Jobac throw you a pity fuck?

God gave us two hands for a reason... and it wasn't to lift the tail of a dead deer and get your jollies. It's bad enough we eat animals but this is just wrong.

One of my little life mottos is, "If I can't tell my mother what I'm doing, then it's wrong." I don't know, maybe this guy can walk up to his mom and say he just had sex with a dead deer. And maybe his mama would say, "That's nice, dear." But then maybe his mama's a little fucked up too.

I was reading in a medical journal... or maybe it was Penthouse, that's a sheep's scootch is the closest thing to a human female's scootch in the animal kingdom. Hold on a second... scootch... scootch... scootch.

OK, I'm really beginning to like saying that. So sheep, huh, how nice. Ladies, isn't it nice to know that if every woman died tomorrow, your man won't be forced into the gay lifestyle? It's great to have choices.

OK, more questions. Why do we need to know this? Is it part of a Harvard study? "Today's field trip is to the St. Louis Zoo. But it's not all fun, this is a class project." Or maybe it was a hazing ritual. "OK man, you want to join our fraternity? Then fuck this sheep. Oh my God, he's doing it… OK, you can stop… hey man… hey stop."

Maybe it was Spring Break. "OK class, I want you to write a report on what you did during Spring Break."

"I had sex with a sheep. It was better than my girlfriend and a lot better than that dead deer last Spring Break."

This is why there are so many laws. Somebody does something stupid, they make a law. They made a burglary law after someone's house got... burgled... robbed.

If you think about it, every state has laws against bestiality. And that means every state has an animal lover that took it to the next level. I'm an animal lover. I don't bang them but they're alright to have around. I guess the difference is how you pet them and what you pet them with.

Do you guys remember around 2003, there were stories about how friendly dolphins were getting? There were about ten stories one summer about men and women getting it on with dolphins. Like because dolphins are cute, it's now socially acceptable to screw dolphins? People just snickered when they read these stories.

You know what? Go ahead. Go out and bang a dolphin. Then come back here and tell us all about it. Go ahead, I'll just wait here... and reload.

The stories I heard get worse, folks.

The next story came from Arkansas. I can't remember the town so I'll tread lightly while I'm there.

A doctor reported that he removed a two inch splinter from the underside of a man's pinga. Would you like to guess what he was screwing?

A maple in bloom. Folks, I love nature but I don't "squirt squirt" love nature. A tree in the spring, when it's in bloom is a beautiful thing. I get it. But I can honestly say that it never gave me a hard-on. That's right. I don't get wood over wood.

A splinter in the pinga is Gods' way of saying, "Stop doing stupid shit. I gave you two hands for a reason."

I mention God here and there because I do believe in a God, but I don't believe he's everywhere otherwise I'd never be able to pee. And if he was everywhere, he'd probably smite this next guy.

A divorced man was upset because his ex-wife was dating other men. How upset? Really upset.

He followed her to a supermarket where she picked up a watermelon for her boyfriend's barbeque. Can you see where this is going? So the ex-husband picked up a watermelon about the same size. Then he took it home, got drunk and... plugged it... it gets worse.

When she left the house, he broke in and switched the melons. At the barbeque, when they cut open the melon, the "slime" was discovered. She knew who did it and took it to the police station.

There, the police cut it up and did DNA tests on it and found sperm from three different men. He had two of his friends make "donations" in it too and they were all arrested.

Now... I can't even get my friends to help me move and this guy has buddies that will fuck fruit for him. It must just be me.

Chapter 5
Sex – C – The Ugly

Sometimes sex gets to the point where you just rather do it yourself. Just knock it out and move on with your life. Most guys do the right hand stranglehold. That's why I'm trying to start a campaign to shake hands with the left hand. It's a lot easier to get a guy to wash his hands then to stop masturbating. Otherwise, no fruit is safe.

I mentioned God before and some of you looked like you knew who I was talking about. I have a feeling God is a real jokester. He is. He put our sexual primes about 20 years apart. By the time women are ready to go, guys are caught up in other things… like making money.

If God really wanted to screw with us, he should let us switch bodies for a day. Men are women, women are men. Then we really get to see how the other half lives. My luck, I'd have my period.

I don't see very much getting done on the planet. Women would be like, "Damn, how do you control this thing? It's like it has a mind of its own."

We've been telling you that for years... now do you believe us? I see women doing a lot of wild things with their pingas but dead animals and fruit are not two of them.

I don't think there would be any surprises as to what guys would do. Ladles, bats, small furniture... anything would be a challenge. I think it's because we're so mature.

The emergency room would be full of things that got "stuck."

Gynecologists would be in for a lot of surprises, "What happened to you?"

"Fire hydrant."

That would be an interesting day. Then men and women would really understand each other. Right now, I don't think we have a clue.

Men don't know what women think about sexually. Even masturbating.

When a guy thinks about a woman "relaxing" herself, we think a locked bathroom door, bubble bath, a few candles, and Barry White softly in the background.

And an absolutely beautiful moment when a woman's mind and body becomes one.. are we close?

We also think that a woman thinking of a guy masturbating is like a monkey furiously yanking the ripcord of a faulty parachute. Ladies, you're actually closer than you think.

If you can't find a partner, there's nothing wrong with "knocking it out" so you can get on with your day. As long as you don't turn that into a freak fest, that is.

Since I don't know how a woman thinks about pleasuring herself, I'll give you the male view. It's bound to be more accurate and funnier.

Before I get into this whole dirty business of "self-love", there's two things that every guy in this room shares...

1. Sometime as a teenager, every guy has bent over and tried to give himself head. We have. You never know, you just may be able to do it.

2. Most guys can improve their sex lives with either a bigger pinga or a smaller hand.

Some people have a real problem with this type of behavior.. like the Catholics. Pronounced cat-licks. I went to Catholic School so I know. I did a five year sentence at Our Lady of Festering Hemorrhoids. The nuns would tell us that Hell was full of "murderers and masturbators." That's quite a club.

Our homeroom nun would tell us at least once a week that if we masturbate, we'll go blind. Luckily I found a loophole... just turn your head. I can't hear for shit in this ear... but I was happy, damn it.

And there was no sex education back then. Dad was no help. The penguins were no help. I learned everything I know from the last place I would have thought to look for information... the library.

I was looking for a book on Babe Ruth. As I walked by a shelf of books, a title jumped out at me. "Sex and You." I left little skid marks as I stopped to look at it. So with my Babe Ruth book covering this ancient porn novel, I read my little heart out. And I got really paranoid whenever someone got within 50 feet of me.. "Go away."

By the time I left the library, I had a severe porn buzz going. "I can't believe people really do that." I remember I didn't believe some of it. Like the part where it said when a man has an orgasm, only about a tablespoon comes out.

As a future scientist, I felt I had to check that theory out. So one weekend, I had some free time so I whipped out a spoon, whipped out a fantasy and went to work. Well, when the work was done, I looked down... and my spoon was empty... apparently it ricocheted off the spoon... and hit a guy in the next pew...

My puberty was brought on early because of Lynda Carter as Wonder Woman. Pure goddess.

And looking back on it, it probably looked so obvious to the rest of the family. Wonder Woman would be doing the opening scenes and then go to commercial. I'd run into the bathroom and lock the door. "Be right there. Don't change the channel."

TV was a great way to understand how lust works. If you were a pre-teen, you either wanted Wilma or Betty on The Flintstones.

When you got older, it was either Mary-Ann or Ginger on Gilligan's Island. There was a lot more room for fantasy on that one but first you had to knock all the men into the volcano. And only after the Professor builds you a still.

Forty years later, that's still a great fantasy. An island, a couple cutie pies, and some hooch. I'd die a happy man.

I think I might be a bit of a prude though. I think sex should be done behind closed doors and masturbation behind bolted doors. But have you seen those commercials late at night for those phone sex lines. You pay four dollars a minute for a girl to talk dirty to you over the phone while you "yank your ripcord."

There are lots of them. I just think it's incredible that guys would pay for this. And there's nothing for women on TV like this because, well, they don't need it... If a woman is thinking about getting laid, they go out and get laid. If a guy is thinking about getting laid, they go out, get shot down, look for a hooker then come home and pay four dollars a minute while they fuck a pillow.

They should put a little truth in these commercials, "For the best piece of ass you can give yourself, dial 1-900-you-loser."

Sex is a BIG business. There are stores that sell everything you need to become a sexual guru... except talent. That's just practice.

So how many of you have gone into these sexual emporiums? You can't miss them. They're usually all pink with three big X's on them. One day, I'd like to see if they sell any double X movies.

You've been in one of those places... no??? Just Buffalo Morgan, huh? Why you lying mothu... you should add it to your bucket list. Sit in the parking lot, have a few drinks and go inside.

They have everything. Dolls with shocked looks on their faces, 55 gallon drums of love lube, all kinds of pinga enlargers from the three dollar brick and a rope to the thousand dollar Sweeba Swaaba 3000. And that comes with a 95% guarantee that it will not rip your organs from your body.

They have costumes, whips and chains. They have dildos that double as Sunday morning softball bats.

The store I went to was out in Vegas and it was so big, it had a little theatre in the back. At the time, I believe they were playing a bestiality movie called, "Our Fine Feathered Friends." Sex with ducks... that's right... duck fucking.

The guys looked like rednecks doing it for beer money. And the ducks... were ducks. Cute, innocent, just looking around, "Say, there are a lot of people here. Is that a camera? You guys making a movie? WHAT THE – quack quack quack quack."

Those kinds of movies must be an acquired taste.

The oddest thing I saw in there was for when you were done doing whatever depraved act you were conceiving, they sold pubic hair shampoo.

They had one called, "Gee, your pubic hair smells terrific." They had another one called, "Spurt."

And if you had dandruff down there, they had, "Head & Testicles."

And we go all through this in the name of love...

Chapter 6
The Echo – Till Death Do We Part Part Part

So is anyone in love here?? When you're in love, it's the greatest feeling. When you get your heart broken, it's the worst feeling. It's like tequila, the night before, it's great to be alive and the day after, someone shoot me.

It's the first time you're in love that you remember. It's lIke your discovery and nobody felt the way you do at that moment. You want to hug and kiss and never leave each other's side.

So beautiful and pure.

I remember the first time I fell in love. I couldn't wait to run home and tell me wife…

Why, yes. I am divorced. How did you guess?

Hold on a second. It's a long path to divorce court and I have to backtrack. One day, we were sitting under a tree together, so happy, it's sickening. Years go by and I'm banging my head on that tree, wondering how I could be so stupid.

OK, let's set up the ground rules.

First - There is a huge difference between love and lust. If you don't know that, you're going to be on a first name basis with the divorce judge.

Second - Anything you don't want your significant other to do then you don't do it. This includes dating (including hookers), drugs, alcohol, gambling excessively, draining the bank account, disappearing for days at a time, threatening the in-laws and selling the children for a Harley.

There's many more but we'll work with these for now.

Third - Lock the bathroom door when you're in there. We all do the same thing but it destroys my illusion of you when I see you wipe your ass.

OK, now that the prep work is done, I'm sure your first question is, "Where do you find love?"

Wrong wrong wrong. You don't find love. Love finds you. Lust you find. You can't swing a dead cat without finding lust. It's behind the counter. It's jogging down the street. It's in a big pink building with the Roman numeral 30 on the roof.

Love is on the inside, you can't see it. First, you have to meet someone. That's the easy part. The hard part is talking. The seed is in the meeting. Talking is what makes love grow... just watch that it's not all fertilizer.

And think before you say something. Here's a good example of a bad example, "I really liked you ever since I first saw you through my telescope."

Stop, stop, stop. No telescopes, binoculars, phone taps, or hidden cameras. A lot of women have a problem with that. I think that falls under the "Honesty" policy most women have.

OK, you said hello. You told her your name and you have about a million things you can be talking about. Here are a few things you might just want to forget about.

Prison - Hey, anyone can make a mistake but if you use Joilet Federal Penitentiary as a second address on job applications, you may want to stick to dead animals and hookers.

Restraining Orders - If you don't know how to leave a relationship gracefully then don't start one. Please see "Prison".

And most women are not impressed if you have two beers then get into a bar fight.

Also if you think it's a good idea to say you're learning a lot from C.S.I. about destroying D.N.A. evidence just in case, she probably won't be calling.

Here's a scenario you don't want to happen to you.

He - "Hi."

She - "Hi... Are you single?"

He - "I am now. I killed my last casual acquaintance because she didn't know what "scrambled fucking eggs" meant."

She - "Oh, I make great scrambled eggs."

He - "Well let's hope you do."

See how blind love can be.

And if the subject comes up, mention ex-wives, ex-girlfriends, and in-laws. Don't go into stories. We all have a past.

I know it seems like I'm picking on the guys but these are just helpful tips.

We know you women are just as insane as us. You're just better at hiding it... **Until it's too late.**

Here's some examples...

Two words... Lorena... Bobbitt... She cut her husband's pinga off, took it for a ride in the car and threw it out the window. I'm willing to bet that he deserved it but she had choices. I do like her attitude though. When that story broke, every guy in a relationship straightened up their act for about a month. Once that first pinga hit the floor, I thought there would be an avalanche of falling pingas. I hear she calls herself Ellen Schwartz now.

The peak of the mountain of insane women that I've known has to be a one night stand in Colorado. A real hottie with a three stooges fetish. As she was riding me, she wanted me to do a Curly impression. So I did the best I could...

NYuck, NYuck, NYuck...
RRUFF, RRUFF, RRUFF...
HE BeBeBeBeBeBe...

All of a sudden, she stops. "That last one was Shemp." Then she climbed off and punched me in the cookies.

So she's sitting on the side of the bed all upset. I said, "Let me get another bottle of vodka and we can talk." She said ok and went into the bathroom. I got dressed and left. I stuck her with the hotel bill, room service and then I finished myself off across her cars' windshield. C.S.I. that D.N.A. bitch. NYuck, NYuck, NYuck.

Ok guys, you've met your dream girl. You saw a movie, had a couple dinners, and she wants to come back to your place.

What should you have done the day before?? Cleaned your place, right.

Because as soon as she walks through the door, she's gonna have to "tinkle" in your bathroom and so may want to clean the candle wax off the toilet tank lid. And we both know it's not candle wax. And eventually, she will too. So tomorrow, buy a scraper.

And if you can't cook anything more complicated than Coco-Puffs... Don't. You can't fake edible food. Buy frozen lasagna, a pre-cut bag of salad, and a bottle of wine. A five year old can handle that.

Hide the porn, throw out empty bottles, and put out a picture of good ole' mom and dad.

I know. It seems like I'm going overboard but trust me, I'm not. I have friends that left porn and drug paraphernalia out and when it's too late, they say, "ahh, oh yeah."

OK, after time, you see if you two are compatible. And you think about your lives together… forEVER… and EVER. And it still seems like a good idea. FOREVER, sorry. So you think about getting married in a year or ten and you will if you can handle the final test.

This is what a week's worth of bitching sounds like condensed into 30 seconds. And if you can deal with this, then you have my blessing to burn your life down anyway you see fit… I mean, get married.

Ready, Set, Bitch…
ThegrassisgettinghighWhyisyourmotherhereagainCharlieandhiswifegoouttodinnerallthetimeStoppokingmeintheback withthatthingYouusedtobringmeflowersAmigettingfatWhyareyounotansweringmeDon'tforgettopickmeuptamponsyouknowwhatkind,rightDoyourselfafavorandrentapornIt'sonlyeightydollarsmoreWillyouaskforfreakingdirectionsWouldIbeaskingyoutotakeashowerifyoudidn'tneedoneTrythatagainandI'llsmackitAsamatteroffact,IdidnailthetoiletseatdownWhen'sthelasttimeyoucleanedthatthingYoushouldcleanitaftereveryuse.

The last two were about a blender you bunch of perverts.

I had a fortune cookie one time that said, "When the honeymoon ends, the static begins." How true.

Getting married is huge. It's a big decision men are not equipped to make.

A friend of mine told me he was marrying his girlfriend because and I quote, "She can suck a golf ball through a garden hose." No thank you. But I will call if I need to steal gas from my neighbor's car. And I'll bet she wasn't born with that talent.

"But she can go all night long." Well, who the hell wants that? Give me two hours of good ole' hardcore and let me get some sleep. And I hope she doesn't snore.

When people ask me why I got married, I give the same answer the survivors of the Titanic gave about why they bought their ticket. "Seemed like a good idea at the time."

And on your wedding day, if you're not 100% sure, look for

omens. Little things in nature that God sends to let you know if it's a good idea or not.

I was drunk. I missed all my omens. Like the six inches of snow... it was June in Jersey. Couple other little things like the minister being taken away in handcuffs or the church caught on fire. Little things like that.

Here's a funny story. In church, all the music was supplied by a boom box... why? The church organist died the night before... Didn't notice that one either. Best man left rings at the house, future father-in-law had diarrhea so he kind of ran his princess down the aisle then ran back to the bathroom. And the new minister spilled his coffee all over the bible... but other than that, went off without a hitch.

My friends screwed around with the boom box. They took out the wedding march tape and played the Jaws theme instead. She came down the aisle to:
dndn...dndn...dndndndn...dndn...dn...dn...

Looking back now, it seemed totally appropriate.

I realized I made a mistake as soon as I sobered up a week later. I began searching the marriage license for an expiration date.

It didn't take long until we realized that the only thing we had in common was rum and sex. That's great for a three day weekend, not 50 years. She didn't like baseball, boxing, or hiking, and I didn't like sitting around with her fat friends, eating ice cream, talking about what kind of an asshole she was married to.

And I remember the last fight we had together as a couple. I was beginning to think it was all me so I went home with the idea to let her choose what we would do that night.

So she's on the sofa and I'm in my chair and I look at her and say, "Uh, Uh, Judy. What do you want to do tonight? We'll do anything you want to do."

And she gave me that answer that every guy hates, "I don't know dear, what do you want to do?"

And you know how a conversation like that can go on for hours, right? So I took the initiative right off the bat... So we're sitting in this Go-Go bar... and she wouldn't give me a dollar. Called my lawyer the next morning.

The first time she brought up the "D" word. I smiled and I laughed. Finally, we agreed on something.

Once your magical marriage turns into a hellish fury, you start to look for ways out. Most times, guys won't bring up divorce but by the time the woman brings it up, we are dancing with joy... on the inside. On the outside, we're like, "Well ok dear, if you think that's best..." On the inside, we're fist pumping and ripping our shirts off, screaming, "Party... Woohoo... Party..."

If any women out there have been seriously thinking about a divorce, knowing nothing is going to change, just tell him. You'll make him very, very happy. He may even kiss you. You only get two very happy days in a marriage. The day you get married and the first day you two start talking about a divorce. I'm sure the day the divorce was finalized, I was pretty ecstatic. I can't remember because I drank tequila for a straight week. And I mean nothing else. Cocoa Puffs and tequila for breakfast, Tequila soup for lunch and tequila tartar for dinner. I got my soul back that week.

Have you ever seen some guy just walking around with some big, dumbass smile for no apparent reason? Chances are, he just woke up from the best sleep of his freaking life. Brought on the day before... he got the "D" word. Life is now worth living again.

But if there are any happily engaged couples out there, ready to commit to this atrocity, please disregard the last five minutes. I'm sure yours will last happily... forever.

AND EVER.

DON'T DO IT, PAL... the baby's not yours.

I'm sorry... where was I?

And for years after our divorce, any time I would run into her at social functions, I'd say something stupid to break the ice when we talked. "Oh hey Judy. Wow, I didn't recognize you without your lawyer… I'm kidding… but hey, you look great… again, I'm kidding."

I had to stop when the kids started to tease her. "Mom, you look funny without your lawyer."

I had to hold my mouth with both my hands to keep from laughing. My God, maybe she was right… Maybe I am an asshole… Nah… I don't see it. She was anal, and not in a good way.

Some people shouldn't be parents and when the kids act like animals, you have to blame the parents. You know, when you're in a restaurant and somebody else's kids are running around and the parents don't seem to care. Their attitude is,

"If we can't have a peaceful dining experience... Why should you?"

Don't you hate that?

I trip the little bastards. What the fuck do they know, they're only three. They still believe they are dumb enough to trip over their own feet. There are some smarter ones that know they've been tripped

but "you're only 3... Who's going to believe you? Hahaha."

And I can't stand people who think letting a baby cry itself to sleep is a good idea. By the 3rd hour of the baby's screaming, I will bring it up. "That fucking kid is killing my buzz. Will you go pick it up or something?"

That's when I usually get asked to leave. Oh, I'll leave... but I'm dancing on the inside.

The funny thing about kids is they're usually reflections of what goes on behind closed doors. If four year old Johnnie is picking little snacks out of his nose then his dad is probably doing the same thing, in his chair, watching the ballgame.

    I was a great dad. I would discipline my kids without them even knowing they were being disciplined. Like, if they ever screwed up big at home, I'd take them out for ice cream. Then I would bet them five dollars I could finish my ice cream before them. So they start shoveling it in. two minutes later, they both have incredibly painful brain freezes. And they're crying, "Boohoo, Daddy. My head hurts." Works on brothers and your kids.

    And as soon as the pain stopped, they went at it again. That's a lot of money to a three and four year old. I couldn't believe I could be so well entertained for just five dollars. I didn't care what they did. I'd give them one of those, "Don't do that again" warnings and they never did. Oh, and they only fell for the ice cream thing three times.

Do you think all those "How to Raise your Child" books has really fucked up the last couple generations.

Man, do I love a good irony.

I think what everyone needs to do at least once is go to the mall and just people watch. It's pretty cool. I added my own little twist to people watching... I get loaded first. If your mall has a bar... and all the best malls have bars... Go get yourself a half dozen Long Island Iced Teas then go sit in the food court and observe.

Sometimes you may see something like someone missing their chair when they sit down. Or an old lady sliding on a pickle. It's all quality entertainment and it's all free. No satellite dishes or cable... and it's all in 3-D... no glasses... unless you need them. If you normally wear glasses then wear them. You don't want to be squinting while you're people watching. Otherwise, you may become the watchee for someone else.

Wow, I really got off course there for a while. I believe I was talking about the beauty of divorce. Yup, there sure are a lot of pros about it and not that many cons. From the side of a male, it's pretty sweet. We get our souls back, our balls and a whole new reason to live.

I guess a con would be, "I'm pissed I didn't think of this sooner." I'm sure a couple cases of beer will make that regret swiftly fade into a deep dark crevice in my mind.

I think I warned you enough about the pitfalls of an enchanting moment in your life. I'm just trying to be the responsible adult. Would I not kick a baby out of the path of a speeding bus? Same concept. You're the baby... and she's the bus...

Now if all I said made no sense and love is eternal and the pigs are a-flyin, I may be enticed to go to your wedding... I mean, if there's an open bar, sure. Why not?

Chapter 7
L.L.A. – Life's Little Anasthesias

I'm going to only say this once... "Thank God for beer." That's the lubrication for a lot of marriages. Just a nice steady buzz that keeps couples from filing restraining orders against each other.

I know alcohol has probably been responsible for a few divorces too. Some guys really can't hold their liquor.

Yeah, can you believe that?

I look at it this way. If it weren't for alcohol, a lot of us wouldn't be here. We were conceived during sloppy drunken sex.

She- "Is the condom on, honey?"

He- "The whaa... I don't haa... yeah baby... it's on."

Know something, this is the greatest country. We had Edison, we invented Rock and Roll, and we landed the first man on the moon. We are the best... thinkers and doers... Lots of brain power. But who thought prohibition was going to be a hot idea?

Back then, workers made $1.50 a day. You played "Rock, Paper, Scissors" to see who was going to eat that day. Have you ever seen a colored picture from the 1920's? Ha, you see? They couldn't even afford color film for their cameras. And you think you're going to take away his nickel beer? What a pinga!!

Thank God for Al Capone... Bet you didn't see that coming. He kept the country lubed up. If they would have just left him alone, he probably never would have killed anyone. He was misunderstood.

One night, I got drunk at a bar that Big Al's ghost allegedly haunts. I didn't see him, but if he is haunting it, he's probably looking for the slut that gave him V.D.

But alcohol is good. When people drink it... they feel better. And I think the government makes a buck or two with... ah... what's the word... oh yeah... taxes. So, everybody wins.

But moderation is key. Especially if you hate hangovers. A hangover is God's way of saying, "You had a great time last night so stop it."

Know what I noticed about drinking? I don't like the drinking habits of the people in my generation. The younger generation, 20 to 25 years old, you party till you drop, wherever that is. And in the morning, there's always someone chipper enough to scramble a shitload of eggs. Now that's a good time.

The older generation, they start partying a little earlier. They get a good buzz going then head to the blue plate special. I was drinking Jack with this one dude who had to be 75... at least. And he was downing a shot of Jack every five minutes. And after a couple hours, I had to go. And if it wasn't for his eyes spinning counter-clockwise, I would have never guessed he'd been drinking.

He was very good at drinking.

My generation, a bunch of paranoid motherfathers. I went to a party two weeks ago, everybody between 40 and 60, so I asked for a second beer and the homeowner shot me this look... and in that look, I could read his mind. And it said, "Hey drunk, if you were in an accident, don't say you were fucking here."

Before I was done the second beer, I had three different people ask me for my keys.

And I would say to them, "Chupa the pinga." Go ahead. Learn a new language.

The Greek Gods drank. You all saw the Hercules cartoon a while ago. Just one big party in Heaven. Did you notice the Satyr… Half man and half goat? What's up with that? Oh yeah, they drank. And the centurions… Same thing but with a horse. Yuck.

But nobody parties like your average college kids. What they learn from Monday to Friday gets erased Saturday and Sunday. Drink till you pass out. And if you fake passing out just so you don't have to drink anymore, the guys would pee on you. It can't be that healthy when you do it two days in a row.

Dad- "Hey Billy, what are you learning in college?"

Billy- "Ah Ah alot dad, just all kinds of crazy and wild things."

Dad- "Oh crap."

In 30 years, they're going to be running this freaking planet. Am I the only one worrying about this? That guy that almost drowned in his toilet last week may be your president someday. That would figure. Didn't we already have a college cokehead as a president? Why not Bluto?

I'll bet you think I went to college. Well... I did, but just to buy pot. And they let me stay for the party.

What was that? When did I do that?

That was 30 years ago and that was last weekend. The weed I used to buy from these dudes, I now buy from their kids.

And I try not to look at the girls in these parties. Because if I'm drinking, then I'm looking. And if I'm looking, then I'm talking. And if I'm talking, then I'm lusting. And you never know when an illegitimate daughter might pop up.

"Oh my God. The things I was thinking about doing to you. I am so sorry. How's your mother?" I did figure out a solution to this horny problem. Just ask them, "Sweetheart, do you know who your daddy is?" I have a feeling my solution is flawed.

I am always looking for ironies and here is one I noticed. Most people that smoke marijuana, can't spell marjuania... that's right, you'll get no help from me.

Yeah, I've been smoking a long time. How long? Let me try out my Rodney Dangerfield impersonation.

"How long? My first bong was made by Fisher Price."

"I smoked out the last dodo bird, ok?"

"We only had raw pot brownies because fire hadn't been invented yet."

I am in what I like to call, "The Marijuana Circle of Life." The first half of my life, I'm hiding my pot from my parents and the second half from my kids.

Pot scares people. I guess it's because it's illegal. It's the biggest cash crop in at least two states, now how does that happen?

Most people that try pot, like it. But some don't. They say they don't get that, "Ain't it great to be alive" feeling. That's ok. There are some people that don't like lobster. Know what I say… "More for us."

I just have one more thing to say about pot… I think. It's a great aphrodisiac.

When you get a shoulder massage, it's like having your soul caressed. And when you move on to more adult activities, you know, you feel EVERYTHING. Best way to describe it, it dulls the toxins that are absorbed into your being just by living. Pure emotion. Just the two of you. Or three, depending on the level of Heaven you are looking for.

I know a lot of you would smoke if you knew where to get it. See, the problem with it being illegal is it can be tough to come by. You have sellers over here and buyers over there. And if the sellers can't wear an, "I'm selling pot" t-shirt, it makes it harder for the buyer to find him.

I can't sell you pot... but I can tell you where to start looking. If you have kids, that's a start. One will usually slip through the cracks and is smoking by 15. If you want it now, you may have to call that cousin of yours. You know the one. He wears the tuxedo t-shirt at all the weddings. And he's fifty.

Your landscaper. If anyone knows about quality bush, it's him. Did you know the only two jobs you don't have to take a drug test for is landscaper and comedian... "HELLO."

Matter of fact, there's a comedy club in El Paso that insists on its comics getting high right before

Barry Hemmerle

they hit the stage. Otherwise they won't book them... Alright, how many of you believed that, come on... See that? I can start my own urban legend.

Know what??? Spread it. Go to work on Monday, tell your colleagues there's a comedy club in El Paso that all the comedians hit the stage high. I mean it, sell it. Oh, then tell them the comics gets paid in weed. It's a good way to test the intelligence of your friends. If your friends follow it all the way... you may want to stop calling these people.

So what do you think? Do medicinal marijuana farmers just love going to work every day? On CNN, they did a bit on the farmers and they're trying to look like scientists with jackets and badges. You know when the cameras left, they cranked up the Rock and Roll and someone ran out for pizzas. I WANT A JOB THERE. Walking with my little hoe, scratching at the dirt.

"It's another great day, Lord."

You know how much I love a great irony, right? This would be beautiful… Ok, we all die and get to meet whatever God you believe in. How I hate being politically correct. And I hope he's just shaking his head back and forth, saying, "I gave you weed so you'll all get along. But you start outlawing that and start making the devils brews. Unfucking real."

And yes, my God curses.

Do you know how high McDonald's stock would skyrocket if they legalized pot? Oh yeah, I have a little pile of money I'm going to dump if it looks like the law's about to change. I'll be a millionaire overnight. It wouldn't be hard to imagine a chicken nugget shortage.

Here's what it would probably sound like if two high dudes were fighting over the last box of Mcnuggets.

"Dude, those are my Mcnuggets."

"No dude, they're my Mcnuggets."

"Oh dude."

"Dude"

"Dude"

"Dude"

"Dude"

That's probably half the reason they won't legalize it. They don't want the world to sound like Tommy Chong.

"Hey man."

"Yo man, what's up, man?"

Even the chicks, "Hey man, is my bra on straight man?"

I made it through 8th grade Spanish class on a strict diet of "Cheech and Chong" movies. If you never saw one of their movies, put that on your bucket list too. Even if you never did any kinds of... fun things... like drinking or getting high, you'll still laugh your ass off.

I did acid one time for a week. It was only supposed to be an eight hour trip. But anytime I'd start coming down, I would eat something. Then one person would divert my attention from the food to him and someone else would put acid on my food. I found this out years later.

They stopped doing it on the four[th] day when I captured all the frogs in the pond and demand that the one that was really a leprechaun turn back into a leprechaun. I know it sounds stupid... but "at the time."

Ever have anyone spring that one out on you? Ok then, I will. "But at the time, it seemed logical. Once I find the leprechaun that I saw
changed into a frog, I get his pot of gold right? Go to the pawnshop and invest in Microsoft. I'd be rich again.

Knowing my luck, I'd invest in Enron... what? Too soon?

I think pot is pretty much legal in Alaska... like 95% legal, you just can't blow shotguns (more street slang) at government officials... while they're on duty.

I'm surprised there's not a billboard behind the "Welcome to Alaska" sign that says, "Full- Go home." My dislike for the cold could easily be bribed by my overwhelming love of pot. I'll just buy an incredibly large sleeping bag where me and my weed can be together... always.

You see what drinking does to you? It softens your freaking head.

So how many of you got high before you got here tonight??? Right, just me. OK, how many of you are going to buy my DVD, take it home, roll a fatty, and watch it?

Hey, we're all whores working to make somebody else rich.

If I happen to luck out and die an old man with my loved ones all around me, know what I want my last words to be? "Do you think there's pot in Heaven?" I'm sure a half hour after I'm gone, they'll be laughing about it.

You know something? I'm going to change my will tomorrow. Anybody I willed anything to has to get high before getting dime freaking one.

You get everyone together in the lawyer's office and hand everyone a big ass joint to smoke. Then the caterers come in and you pig out on anything you want. Then when you straighten up, you take your money and get the fuck out.

You can screw with people and be helpful. Like my one relative that isn't very smart. Tell him he gets $1000 every time he finishes a New York Times crossword puzzle. See? Even in death...

I went to a town meeting one night and they were talking about the golf fees going up again. So I segued in, "Speaking of green grass, Mr. Mayor. Is there any way you can legalize pot in this town and just make other drugs more illegal?"

And that was the last town meeting I was ever invited to.

I think I'd make a great mayor. First... I'd declare our town is breaking from the U.S. to become its own country within a country. And I'll call it... Buffalo... I can't call it Morgan. I've already heard of a town called Morgan so Buffalo it will be.

"Oh, Mr. President, remember those tax dollars you used to get from us? Well that's all over with. Now get back to your own country."

And you better believe were bringing back that wonderful crime deterrent... corporal punishment. After we snap a couple limbs on live TV, our crime rate will drop through the floor.

And if you think you will have freedom as soon as you cross the border, my army of ninjas will see to it that you won't make it.

OK, now who wants to be a marijuana farmer? I need a lot of volunteers. You know that commercial where the guy says, "Beef... it's whats for dinner." We can add a tail line. "Weed... it's your fucking salad."

Someone would probably come up with a marijuana cookbook, and I don't mean "Cooking with Pot." That'd be too small of a book. "Just use whatever recipe you like... and throw in a handful of pot.

Dad- "Honey, what are you making for dinner?"

Mom- "Your favorite dear, pot pot roast."

Family- "YEAH."

Say good-bye to that B.L.T., it's now a B.M.T.

And know what tastes better than a big bowl of Cocoa Puffs and milk?

Cocoa puffs and pot and milk!!!

Hey, how do you know?? You never tried it and by the third spoonful, you may think that's the tastiest thing you ever ate.

What I mean is a cookbook with special munchies menus.

Sicilian pizza with Milk Duds.

Elvis was good at it. That peanut butter and banana sandwich, its killer.

"Room service?" "I'll have a bowl of dark chocolate covered Cocoa Puffs, pot, and some milk, please? I know it's my third bowl but I like it."

Maybe I won't get involved with politics. I'd have a town with a bunch of stoned cripples in it. No offense if you are stoned and/or crippled.

So I was reading the Bible yesterday… Oops, sorry. Not that Bible. I meant "High Times" and in this magazine, they quote the Bible (yes, that Bible) at least a dozen times. One quote they said I didn't believe. So in this strange motel room I found myself in, I looked it up in the Bible, and there it was, just like they said.

Hey, you know what "High Times" has that "Home & Garden" or those other mags don't have??? A centerfold!!!

And if you have a real lust for "God's favorite flower," you have to see the centerfold each month. And just when your smoking fantasies end with the May issue... Here comes June, dressed in purple, pink, and gold, and what appears to be shimmering silver fuzz dispensed from the dreams of yesteryear... I've seen live plants. Some of my friends are... multi-tasking and it's amazing. I walk into the basement/farm and if it wasn't green, it was gold. Do you know what my last two thoughts will be before I die?

Shaking Eric Clapton's' hand and walking through this guy's basement.

Sorry kids... you're 3A and 3B, I swear.

My kids discovered pot a few years back so occasionally I'd pop into their room while they're there. I'd go into authority mode, "My God, what is that smell?" and it was always in their sock drawer. "Look at that. I am going to flush that. Don't you ever bring that here again... Goodnight." (Wink)

Then I'd flush an empty toilet and run back to my room, "Oh my, smell this... this has to be... some good shit... GO TO SLEEP IN THERE... wow."

And every month, "High Times" ignores my letter. "Next month, please include a 3-D centerfold and a couple scratch and sniffs."

If I ever ran this dirty, stinking planet, every magazine, no matter what they're advertising, has to have at least half a dozen marijuana scratch and sniffs in their magazine.

Dude- "What's with the hunting magazine, Bill? You don't hunt."

Bill- "Maui WoWee scratch and sniff."

Dude- "ALRIGHT."

Getting back to my political career, I do have just one last thought on my mayorship. If all we did was farm, we could sell whatever we don't smoke or eat. After our first harvest, we'll be richer then Japan. And we won't give it a fancy name like Columbian Gold or Panama Red. A nice simple name, "Medicinal" that will confuse the shit out of everybody.

As much as I like pot, I think it is beginning to affect my memory. Last night, I got high and I lost my bag of Doritos. I looked for a half hour.

Know where I found them? In my other hand.

Chapter 8
I'll Take Five Losing Lottery Tickets, Please

So how many of you are doing what you said you wanted to do during high school? See, a couple. Most of us didn't have a clue. We felt around blindly, in the dark, until something felt right.

And here I am. And to keep myself humble, my little ritual before I hit a stage is I'll say to the manager, "Hey boss, can I have a couple beers while I work tonight?" They always say, "Sure."

I guess only comics and beer tasters ever get to say that. But I do it for all of you.

One of the great things about being a comic is meeting some wonderful people. Some of the managers like, "Phil" tonight. He treats me like gold and all he asks for is a joke.

He just loves this joke... I don't know why but here you go, Phil. "What's the difference between a pinga and a dick? A pinga is used for urination and procreation and a dick is what stands behind it... Thanks. Simple minds, simple pleasures.

My first real job was a farmer when I was twelve and not the good kind. That was real work. Farmers do not get the respect they deserve. I'd be pretty fucking hungry if somebody wasn't growing my food. I live in Jersey. How many freaking tomatoes do you think I can eat?

Ok, so if farmers have one of the hardest working jobs, who has the smartest jobs? A lawyer... has to have a quick mind during questioning. A doctor... has to be very exact with his tools.

I think the smartest is... a dentist!

You look surprised... sure. The lawyer and the doctor you might see once in a lifetime but a dentist tells you he needs to see you every six months. And there's always something wrong... right? You can never floss enough for those people.

It's not us... it's them. They have brainwashed us into brushing our teeth three times a day. And to use toothpaste. Toothpaste tastes like candy. Candy is made of sugar...DIABOLICAL.

They must have done a time study and it averages a dental problems every six months. You people are so clever but the party's over. We're all going to start brushing with olive oil. Olive oil fixes everything. And then we're going to do some tests of our own. I'm sure we'll find something a little bit better than "SUGAR." Know something?

It'd be great if a scientist came up to me during a show and said, "This man is right."

And that whole dental empire of lies comes crashing down. Then in a couple of months, you may get that rare opportunity that comes just once in a lifetime… Hiring your dentist… to cut your grass. And you can follow him around, yelling at him, "Thanks for all the lies, Dave.

You're such a pinga, Dave."

After we win that class action suit against you that you can't afford to pay, the next time you cut our grass, we will be able to throw food at you… "Ok Dave, what'll it be? Jersey tomatoes or Jersey corn?" Hey, I still live in Jersey.

Once the evidence starts rolling in, we'll have you… Hey, you people still scare my people. Anybody who's not a dentist is afraid of you. And stop being so stingy with the anesthesia. A couple hits before we got started could really help your public image.

Know what it is? They use you to build their self-esteem. They tell you they're your dentist for life. I told my dentist I was going to shop around and he was shocked.

"But, but I'm your dentist… forever."

"No dude, you're too expensive."

"Oh yeah? And where will you go?"

"Well, you see the top of the escalator there? That building next to the Old Navy store…

Yeah, that flashing neon Dentist sign. I'll try there."

"You're bluffing…"

"Last week... He gave me his card... huh."

"Ok, twenty dollars off."

"DEAL."

Oh crap, I forgot to ask. Are they any dentists in the audience tonight??? Well, you may have wanted to take a pee five minutes ago.

Damn, I always do that. Wait, there's a message coming through the loud speaker.

"Will all gynecologists report to room 311. It's an emergency."

See ya fellas. I'll hold the show up for you... No, I'm not... is he gone?

Ok... ladies, I'm investigating these people too. And I'm surprised I'm the one that figured it out. A doctor, "a gynecologist" will tell you that he or she can find out everything that's wrong with you in a simple blood test.

Then why get... intimate? Do they consider that part of their payment? I'd like to question one and get the truth...

"If it's all in the test tube, what's with the rest, man?"

"Hey man, we're all dudes... Except Betty... She's just gay."

Well??? Well???

Me and my ex-wife were always fighting about hers'. It was like a cult. You can't even say the name... you had to spell it. I was walking by my ex, who was on the phone... a real telephone and this is what she said. "I can't do lunch tomorrow, I have to go to the O.B.G.Y.N. tomorrow." So I turned around and said, "Yes honey, the obgyn... scootch is getting her check-up. I can spell... I'm not an idiot.

A couple weeks later, I did the same to her. I was on the phone when she walked by, "I'm sorry Gene. I can't make it Saturday. I have a D.E.N.T.I.S.T. appointment." She turned and stared at me. "Ha, you don't like it when people do it to you, huh?"

Ok, they're coming back, "Ok, so after farming got to be too much tomato picking and watching the animals mating, I needed a structured job. So I became a chef in a Scottish restaurant… you might have heard of it… McDonalds. That was the worst 7 years of my life.

And it ended badly. I… got fired… from McDonalds. I didn't think that was possible.

And it wasn't my fault. I was sitting around during my break and I was looking at my McPaycheck… I said, "This McBlows." So I went up to the McManager… McMike… and said, "I want a McRaise."

He said, "McNo."

So I gave him the McFinger.

And he McFired me.

What a McPinga.

But remember what I said about the "Law" changing? Money, money, Ka-ching.

Not all McDonalds are the same. They are usually very clean except the one I found in Washington. There were condiments on the floor and my bag had blood on it. On the wall, they had pictures of "Employee of the Month."

For the last four months, it was a picture of the "Caution, Wet Floor" sign.

I thought about being a cop but I couldn't just smile with some of the shit they have to put up with.

"You know, I've been chasing you for six months and I bet I averaged about three hours of sleep a night because of you."

"Really, well fuck you."

"Hey Pat, can you pull out that plug next to the camera?"

WHAP!

"Ok, plug it back in."

"Hey, what'd you do? Slip on the floor?" Where's our "Caution, Wet Floor" sign? "He's been late three times this month. He's never gonna make 'Employee of the Month.'"

I have a lot of respect for policemen and policewomen. I tried to be a cop once. I was under the impression that after a big pot bust, we were allowed to skim from the pile. Can you believe it? They have a law against that too? I didn't even pass the physical. Well, I threw up after eating only 7 donuts. I had no idea they were so strict.

Ah crap. Are there any cops here tonight? No offense, but you make me nervous. I was at a party last year and the hostess introduces me to her friend Jim. And as I'm reaching to shake his hand, she says, "Jim is a State Trooper."

And just as our hands met, I felt my mouth say, "Oh crap." Me and my wonderful first impressions. Now I can't drink because he might wait for me in the parking lot.

"Leaving so soon? I better follow you to make sure you get home."

"No, no... I have a ride... Here comes my bus." I'll tell you one thing about cops...

They throw a hell of a beef and beer. No wonder they're all a hundred pounds overweight. They eat well and they have guns. They don't have to chase you.

"Hey Pig, bet you can't catch me." (Pulls his gun.) BANG! "I'll bet I can."

There are just some jobs I can't do for various reasons.

The person that peels those little shrimp and puts them in a can… too tedious.

Hot tar roofing… smell makes me vomit.

Even as a kid, I didn't want to be a gynecologist. Hey, for every Jessica Alba that comes through your door, you may have to look at a thousand of the strangest scootches that will ever haunt your dreams. No offense.

Not everybody shaves it. I'm sure some haven't seen a pair of clippers since the "70's". I'm pretty sure a scootch looks better without a ponytail.

Guys can just clean up… We do clean it up down there, right guys?

And some of us would shave but where would we stop? You can't just shave around your pinga. Your stomach has hair, shave it. Ok, your chest has hair, shave it. Are you happy? Now I look like a twelve year old. A twelve year old with a big pinga.

As far as acting jobs, I'd do erectile dysfunction commercials if the price was right but I couldn't be an actor for the Renaissance Faire.

If they paid enough, I could maybe be the drunken blacksmith or the drunken court jester or a drunken knight. See where I'm going with this? I could see it.

If I didn't hate crime as much, I'd feel sorry for those prisoners picking trash up on the side of the highway.

"How much are we getting paid for this?"

"$5 a day."

"Say what? Now who's drunk in public?"

Whatever you do for a living, I hope it makes you happy.

Living a good life should be easy.

1st, you spend 1/3 of your life in bed, have a comfortable bed.

2nd, Pick a career doing something you like doing. That's another 1/3.

3rd, Keep the last 1/3 simple and easy to manage.

I might try all that someday.

Chapter 9

All I want for Christmas is a Cannon Bolted to the Hood of my Car

You guys have been a great audience tonight. I raise my glass to you, salute.

Wow, that's a lot of drinkers. Where are our designated drivers tonight?

One… and two. Wow, unless you have a couple double decker buses out there, you guys are going to make a lot of trips back here tonight.

Drunk driving is no joke and if you think those mints in your pocket will sober you up, think again.

If you get pulled over and that window goes down, know what the cop smells??? Beer and Tic Tac's… Or tequila and Big League Chew.

But a piece of gum the size of a football wouldn't stop the beer-lip comments of an old buddy of mine. He'd always have enough lip to say something stupid.

And man, he liked to argue...

So we're coming home from a club one night, he's driving and he keeps hitting the yellow line.

The third time he hit it, I said, "Dude, stop hitting the line."

"I'm not."

"You are."

"No man, this is hitting the line."

So he's just driving on the yellow line on purpose. So I'm like, "Dude, you're gonna get pulled over."

He's like, "No I won't, dude."

All of a sudden, the car that's been following us flips on his lights.

So he looks at me and says, "Dude, it's a cop... I'm gonna run."

As he's about to stomp it, I must have squealed, "No" like a little school girl. He looks at me and stomps the brake. We both flew into the windshield. Before I could say the "F" word, the cop rammed us from behind. I meant the car. And I get bumped into the backseat. Now I'm bruised and pissed.

The cops have our doors open in about three seconds, "You alright? You alright?" "I'm alright but if you want to shoot that asshole driving, I'll look the other way."

So I'm thinking, "Great, he's drunk driving but they hit us. We just might get out of it."

So my friend, who was no longer my friend, starts his lips to flapping.

"You stupid cop, I'll sue the city then get you fired."

So the cop walks over to him and says, "What's that smell on your breath??? Alcohol!"

"Yeah but your breath smells funny too. It smells like semen... animal semen..." Then he looks at me and says, "Harold and Kumar, dude."

So the cop spins him around to cuff him and he says, "Hey man, what crawled up your éclair today?"

Another cop comes pulling up and they walk him to it and all I hear is, "I didn't call you an asshole, I called you a whole ass."

Now, I just wanna go home. And in his last ravings, I remembered why I was friends with him. He was tough... and stupid. Before they closed the back door, the cop says to him, "Because you have a big mouth, I'm going to put you away for a while."

So he says back to the cop, "I'll be out in four hours banging your mother."

Never saw him again... Strange.

So be careful if you're drinking tonight. I got pulled over once out in Vegas, driving to a club. Bang. There's the lights.

Can you guess the first two words out of my mouth? I'll give you a hint. The first word was "Oh". Yeah, you got it.

So I stop, he comes to the window, smells the Big League Chew and tells me to get out of the car. So he asks if I've been drinking. I said yes. He said, "How much?" I said, "I don't know. My mother wasn't there to count them."

So we start the tests, stand on one foot, touch your nose. By the way, I can't do these tests sober. I even screw up the alphabet half the time. After I do the alphabet for him, he says, "Ok, now backwards." Do you know why a cop would ask you that? Because only a drunk would try it. Or a comic with a lot of time on his hands.

So I lean against my car, "Z,Y,X,W,V,U,T,S,R,Q,P,O,N,M,L,K,J,I,H,G,F,E,D,C,B,A."

And the cop's head exploded.

But this is America. We only have what, 20... 25 letters. I'm glad I wasn't in China. They have like, 5000 letters or symbols. And with my luck, I'd get that one cop that says, "Ok, now backwards."

"Oh fruck."

In some Arab nations, you can get the death penalty for drinking and driving... no joke. You better hope a sympathetic cop pulls you over. Maybe he'll let you make a deal. "You can take your chances in court or you can let my camel have its way with you… your choice."

The same way some people shouldn't be parents or pet owners, some people shouldn't drive. Just because you fooled a driving examiner for five minutes doesn't mean you're a driver.

I live in Jersey and we have circles. The normal driver maneuvers them with no problem. I take a lawn chair and a 6-pack there and watch the abnormal ones try it.

It's amazing what a little common sense and a turn signal will help you accomplish.

I have a C.D.L. I know stupid when I see it. And I will help anyone that needs help but the last snowstorm, some knuckle-head in a pick-up truck flies by me. A mile later, he's on his side in a ditch and I did not help him but only because I was laughing too hard. Right now, I'm looking at all the states for a place to retire and driving is part of the criteria.

I want the taxes to be low. Not a lot of traffic so I can get my motorcycle license. And it also has to be legal to bolt a small cannon on the hood of my car. I will personally keep slow drivers out of the left lane and the folks that forgot their car has a turn signal won't forget again.

I was a biker for years but I always wore a helmet. Not because I wasn't confident with my riding but because so many people think they own the highway and just drift from lane to lane. "Oh, were you there? I didn't see you." "You didn't look, asshole."

I think we can save a lot of lives every year if we put huge bumpers made of rubber on our cars. You wanna drive like you're sleeping now we're ready for you. Simple solution to a difficult problem. When I first started, I knew I was a lousy driver. I used to kick on the cruise control and jump in the back seat for a nap... You learn.

Chapter 10
A Big Pile of Conglomafux

A lot of times after a show, somebody will come up to me and say, "I wanna be a comic."

I say, "Go for it."

But remember, you have got to know you'll have to suffer for your craft. You will have to do shit you'd never thought you had to do to prove you can.

Like heckle a wedding. Go to a wedding and get involved.

Priest- "Does anybody deny David's purity?"

You- "He porked the bridesmaid last night."

Priest- "Or Jessica's purity?"

You- "She's carrying the best man's baby."

Now, CAN YOU DO THAT? I did one better.

Know what I did??? I heckled… my own wedding… oh yeah. The priest looked out at the congregation and said, "Does anybody see reason why this couple should not be wed???" And nobody said a thing.

So the priest looks right at me as I said, "Don't I get a fucking vote!" and I forgot I was on a mike and everyone heard it. My sisters' daughters' embryo heard it. So I'm trying to play it off like, "Haha, I'm just doing comedy. It's like… my thing. My side of the family thought it was hysterical.

So remember, if you do this… you may not get out alive but that's just part of the price… of being a comic.

Second… You have to scare a small child… at a funeral. You may want to try... ventriloquism. I had tremendous success with that one.

At all funerals, the parents want their child to go up and say goodbye to grandpa. And there always seems to be someone standing up there at the casket... Be that someone... and scare the living shit out of one of your nieces or nephews.

Jimmy- "Goodbye Grandpa. I love you."

You as Grandpa- "Jimmy... don't let them bury me... I'm only sleeping."

All of the sudden, little Jimmy jumps into the box and starts bitch slapping Grandpa, telling him to wake up.

Now who has the freakish child? And third... you must go to a Bris and make a big fuss over the size of the kid's pinga.

Just before the ceremony starts, say, "Oy, look at the size of this kid's schmetson. Just the foreskin, he wouldn't miss half that snake... If I was a sleazy chick, I'd say, 'I would do you right now.'"

And pictures... lots of pictures... before, during, and after. And don't forget a picture of Uncle Hemes as he runs down the aisle, waving the foreskin overhead. We have no idea why he does that.

And if you could do just those three things... you may get invited to... an open mike.

And as the M.C. gets ready to do your introduction, you'll think about escaping to the street. It doesn't seem like such a good idea anymore.

All of a sudden... it's real.

"The most exciting place this next comic's been is his mother's womb... Keep it going for... "Buffalo Morgan."

"Ah crap."

My first word on stage was actually a fart. Yeah... Check your trivial pursuit game; I'm sure it's on there.

So this is how it happened... The M.C. called my name, I leaped on stage, as I stepped toward the M.C., I cut loose then shook his hand and my first words into a mike was, "Oh my God... Can you smell that?" I got a good laugh with an ad-lib. I'm gonna be a star... What's my next line??? Oh crap, I forgot my act.

"Dude, get the fuck back up here." That got another good laugh.

So I look at it this way. I was on stage for 20 seconds and had 16-17 seconds of good laughter. That's a good percentage. I killed that night.

See, you have to talk yourself into a lot of things before you hit the stage.

Oh yeah, one more thing. When you hit the stage, say how nice the audience is. They seem to like hearing that bullshit... no offense... Say something nice.

But the best part after you survive that first show, good or bad, you're no longer one of them.

You're one of us. You are an entertainer... No matter how badly you sucked the first time... the next 5000 shows are a cakewalk. Oh yeah and here's the best part. After six or seven years, you start to get paid. Isn't that exciting?

Oh my, I remember my first $2 gig. To celebrate, I went out and had a beer... and used the $2 for a tip. Money well spent.

And yes, if you enjoy sleeping on any old stranger's sofa and panhandling all day then come on. There's always enough room for another million... fucking... comics. Sorry.

Ever hear of "Fight to the Death" pizza? That's when seven comics order a pizza and they fight to the death for the last slice.

That's why it's good to be a comic mentor, like me. So when the rest of us are betting on a winner, I'll have the edge.

Buffalo- "So Jeff, what did you do before comedy?"

Jeff- "I was an up and coming boxer. I tore a knee muscle and the doctor told me I had to quit."

Buffalo- "That's a shame. Do you ever work out anymore?"

Jeff- "Oh yeah, I work out every day."

Buffalo- "Well that's good. Say, don't say anything about this boxing thing to anyone ok? It might throw people off."

Jeff- "Ok."

Buffalo- "Just say you paint houses."

Jeff- "Ok."

Buffalo- "We're having pizza for dinner. Do you like pizza, Jeff?"

Jeff- "I love pizza."

Buffalo- "I wanna bet $1000 on this man."

Jeff- "And if I can't have a second slice, I might have to kill somebody..."

Buffalo- "And my soul... I'm betting $1000 and my soul on this man. What is the going rate for a soul these days?"

That scares people... selling your soul. How many of you would sell me your soul for $5? Just write your name on a cocktail napkin, apostrophe S and the word "soul." And I will give you $5 for it... Nobody wants to sell? What, do you think I collect souls??? No, I sell them on E-Bay. You'd be amazed what a stranger would pay for a soul. How else can I make $1000 bets on pizza fighting?

Over the last five years, I've had to sell my soul three times on E-Bay just to cover the mortgage. Don't worry about me. I have my original soul in a safety deposit box, in a bank, in El Sagundo. Who is gonna even think my soul is in El Sagundo??? I mean, except you guys. And as you listening to my calming voice, I am slowly stealing your soul, as I speak… Ok, who flinched? I'm not stealing your soul but there are people out there that want your soul. They will buy your card with your soul on it, take it home, and rub it in their pants… It's sex… with your soul. And how do I know this??? There's a Soul Rapists Anonymous club around the corner from my house. I had to go one night because I feel as a comedian, it is my responsibility to keep you updated on all the freakiness that pops up now and then. So watch out for soul rapists.

Oh yeah and they're building a Subway shop right across the street from my house. So from different rooms from my house, I can see three different Subway shops. Stop building these things everywhere or build them in better locations like split an office with the D.M.V.

Your number 257 and they're on three... and they're closing in five minutes. Do I want a pre-21st century gumball or oohh, a meatball marinara with pepper jack cheese and banana peppers?

I'm like a business genius... well maybe not but that's what I'd like to see happen. Because they do that alot now. Like put a Long John Silvers and a Taco Bell together. That's ok but I'd like to see a small town bar on one side and a Chinese buffet on the other. I'd be back up to 300 pounds in a month. I lost a lot of weight because of something someone said to me in a buffet one night.

I was 302 pounds and most of it was my Irish hog gut. I was big. Well, another "Big" guy comes over to me and says, "That was a brilliant performance."

I thought he was talking about my show the night before. He wasn't. He said, "I've never seen anybody eat that much at one time, dude. I was done eating an hour ago but I had to keep watching you. The manager has been biting his fingernails waiting for you to leave.

And that little innovative thing you do, two forks in one hand… fantastic. You're like a swarm of locusts. Locust, dude. That's what I'm going to call you. Locust."

So the next day, I developed my own diet. Anything I eat or drink will be sprinkled with Metamucil. Food went in and out so quick, I could still identify it. In three months, I lost 100 pounds. That was two years ago. And just last week, I had my first solid bowel movement in two years. I'm sorry, is that TMI?

Losing weight is tough and I was in Vegas for six of those weeks with all those buffets there. I was always carrying a big container of Metamucil into those places. As long as I sprinkled it, I could eat it. I just had to make sure I wasn't working the next day. You do need recovery time.

And there were a couple times I thought I wasn't gonna make it home in time.

I'd run like a penguin from the front door to the bathroom. And I'd say a little prayer to whomever you think made all this. I'm sorry but I'm so tired of people fighting about the name of the great creator.

And I'm not crazy about God's name. "God." God is what he is, not his name. Like a car mechanic is not named "Mechanic." It's Steve or Bill or Tracy.

God means he's the creator of... whatever.

I think they should come up with a huge committee with representatives from each religion that calls the great creator "God." And they all have to come up with a name and why it's their choice.

I think the Catholics would pick "Freddy." So this way, they can scare you when you're awake and you're sleeping. Ring around the Rosie, folks. But I got the perfect name. It's universal and loved and universally loved. HE'S MY GOD AND YOUR GOD, HERE HE IS... GOD ELVIS.

"Thank you... Thank you very much."

And if you take the lord's name in vain, God Dammit still flies.

You will not take the king's name jokingly and say Elvis dammit.

I'm willing to bet the pizza money I'll win tonight that when the "Civil War II" gets going. It's going to be because a Yankee went to Graceland and wrote "Fuck Him" on the bathroom wall.

You have to watch those southern folks. They hit you with that southern hospitality and you're gone. "Y'all want some of this? Y'all want some of that?"

"Quit trying to soften me up with extra hush puppies. I know what you're planning."

That's strange. My psychiatrist says I'm no longer paranoid. I better cancel his last check.

He's court ordered... long story. And I have to pay him $200 an hour. So I'll screw with him.

Last week, I was telling him about my day. The first three sentences were English. The next sentence was in Spanish. And then two more sentences in English.

So he asks me why I spoke in Spanish. I said, "I don't know how to speak Spanish."

He said, "But you just did."
I said, "No I didn't."
He said, "Are you sure?"
I said, "Si."

It must have taken this guy forever to get his license. He's so stupid. Our first meeting, to build my confidence in him to "share myself", he made a confession to me that he should have left into the farthest reaches of his brain.

He says he's compulsive about his stuff. He said, "Everything in my office is in its perfect place."

How interesting.

Next week, I brought him a coffee. Two creamers, three sugars, and one roofie.

So when he fell asleep, I moved everything in his room. Furniture, pictures, and every book and paper. I heard he cancelled two days of appointments "putting everything in its perfect place."

I think everyone goes through a compulsive stage. Mine was when I was 8. I had an obsession with my dad's driving. As we drove by a telephone pole, it's like a finish line at a drag race and if someone was coming the other way... we had to beat him... we HAD to. So I'm like, "Dad, hurry up, we're losing."

And one day my dad said something to me that changed my life forever. He said, "Shut the fuck up." And in that surly phrase, I became a man. No longer did light pole racing interest me. From that moment on, I was preparing for the working world and sex.

Do you know what way of life this country could never get behind? Cannibalism. Do you people realize how many problems this solves for people?

1st- Less cemeteries means more golf courses.

2nd- There's starving because of too many people. Duh.

3rd And people will start to treat you nice so you don't eat them. It's harder to eat a friend. "I can't eat Dave because he let his wife stay with me for a couple nights. So I can't eat either one of those people. The mail always comes on time so that person is safe. Hell man, I might go back to cows and chickens."

It'd do wonders in the judicial world.

If you knew you could be sentenced to be an entrée, you might go back to your fast food job and apologize for being a dumbass.

Could you imagine a politician pushing for cannibalism? "So when you vote on Tuesday, remember prop-27 to vote yes on ahh… a new food source. You let me worry about the details. After all, I am your senator… you can trust me."

"Oh crap, he used the T word. Someone is gonna have to follow the senator day and night for a while. Mother, should I trust the government?

I'm only trying to help."

So how many of you have a bucket list? You know, things to do before you... check out.

Well, if going to a nudist beach is on there, you may as well scratch that off right now. Some friends invited me so what the hell. It sounds good on paper. Maybe it will be like the French Riviera. Guess what? It wasn't. I couldn't grind hot sand into my eyes quick enough. It was horrible and I was scared and I wanted to go home.

Maybe it was a special day like "Fat and Fuzzy Friday", "One Ton Wednesday", or "Sun and Saggy Saturday."

One guy had a boil on his ass the size of a softball... and he kept touching it. Absolutely no shame.

Up until this point in my life, I wasn't judgmental. But come on. If your husband needs two hands to move one of your breasts so you can lotion up, it's time to discover vegetables.

No wonder dolphins are being molested. It's hard to tell the aquatic life from the sunbathers.

That's why they invented clothes... so the rest of us could eat.

The girl that took me there was a hot little redhead I dated for a long time. As we pulled into the parking lot, she said, "And remember, don't stare."

If I stared, I think I would have barbequed my retinas.

She was your typical hot-tempered Irish woman. And headstrong.

One night she insisted that I give her a nickname. So red hair,

"Ruby?"

"No"

"Red?"

"No!"

"Honey?"

"Oh, you're not even trying."

So I said, "How about pest?" and she loved it.

I felt bad for her. Her monthly thing was apparently very painful. I was never surprised when that started.

During one of those, "BAD" days, I guess I wasn't sympathetic enough. She pushed me away and screamed, "You don't know how easy you guys have it. You don't know how lucky you are."

I said, "I could be luckier. I could be deaf."

That got the coffee cups flying. How I love to play with fire. And this is not the three Stooges chick. This is a completely different crazy then that chick.

I don't know why I keep saying chick tonight. I just don't feel like saying woman or girl. Hey, if I feel like the 50's, slanging it up, I will.

This is my show and I will chick it up. I may talk about how crazy women are... and I'm not wrong. But sometimes I think the being that wired my head may have been fresh out of trade school.

There are times I have to give the voices inside my head a mental milk bone just to get them to shut the fuck up. "Hey guys, since there's no air on the moon, could a fart still have sound?" That'll keep them busy.

You guys hear voices, right? It's not just me... right? Ever argue with yourself? And I don't mean your conscience. My conscience is a real tight ass. He won't let me have any fun.

I mean argue with just one of the voices... like it just won't shut up.

"Is all the oil really the result of four billion years of mulch?"

"I don't know."

"When we die, is God Elvis gonna have a D.V.D. of every time you touched yourself?"

"Shut up."

"Buffalo, should I trust the government?"

"Don't sing."

"Doesn't the Chinese yin yang symbol look pornographic?"

I read that you can quiet your mind with meditation. I tried it but the only thing it did was help me hear them better.

Me- "I am sitting, I am silent, I am one."

1st voice- "Hey buff, what are we doing for lunch? I vote sushi."

2nd voice- "We had sushi Tuesday. How about a cheesesteak?"

3rd voice- "Hello, have you considered a salad?"

1st & 2nd voices- "Shove your salad. Buff, can't you shut #3 up? He sucks."

Me- "Ok, beer it is."

So yesterday, me and the voices were discussing how come everyone had to die . It doesn't seem fair. If you accomplish everything you're supposed to do in this life, you should be able to just slide into the next plane of existence without dying here first. And they give you an "I Survived Death" merit badge. Knowing you have to die takes all the fun out of making a billion dollars if you only have to give it back at the end.

What is that saying, "The first million is the hardest?" That person knew what they were talking about.

I think I'll get that one millionth dollar when I open my birthday card for my 100th birthday. And I'll probably fade to black as I touch it. But it can all turn around just like that.

The lottery Elvis can look down and say, "Know something? I always liked this dudes' haircut. Let's let him win tonight."

"Ok, yeah it is nice hair."

Then I can follow my dream… being a beer connoisseur. If not the lottery, I can get knocked over by a bus. I hear there's a lot of money being a "professional victim." Slip and fall in a casino, Ka-ching. But it has to look good. They have cameras everywhere. Even in the bathrooms. I heard that from a very reliable schizophrenic.

And under the new cannibalism law, if you get caught, you can be sentenced to be an entrée at the midnight buffet.

Speaking of bad meat, how long do you have to stand in line before it's not considered fast food anymore? Remember the uproar when somebody found a finger in their chili at a fast food place? See that? This country is not ready for such a radical food source. And whose finger was it?

Probably not the minimum wage cook. I'll go with the chili maker from a foreign country. Either he had leprosy and it fell off or he owed money and it was macheted off.

I had a rare day that I didn't have anything to do last week. Those are great, aren't they? You can do anything you want. I wanted to take a nap. No, it wouldn't be a waste. I'd remember that nap for 50 years. I'd be hanging with my grandkids. "Hey, did I ever tell you about the nap I took back in 2011? That was a great time." Grandson- "What did you dream, Grandpa?" Me- "Hell if I know. You kids want a beer?"

And that would be another crazy story for ole' Grandpa Morgan.

Talking to my great grandchildren.

"Did I ever tell you about when your parents were kids, I used to give them beer. They would walk into walls and trip over things. I laughed my ass off. I'm surprised you little bastards are normal... Want a beer?"

Well I didn't get my nap. Now what the hell am I going to tell them about? "How I planned a nap in 2011 but it failed."

I could see these little kids making an "L" with their fingers on their foreheads.

So I will plan another nap… Perhaps next fall.

So what I ended up doing was pounding down a big bag of Doritos and watched "Journey to the Center of the Earth." Do you know the story?

Some explorers go down a cave and find another world under the surface. It has dinosaurs and cave people. Always thought that was a cool story. But how long do you think it would take the powers that be to turn it into a theme park? How about Jurassic Park? That's a great name… oohh.

But like a carnival atmosphere. The kids can ride a brontosaurus. The parents can watch a Tyrannosaurus Rex cage fighting. And all the people that lived there peacefully now have a job.

And if you didn't want a job, you would just disappear. Later, you would reappear in the Le Brea Tar pit chili. And the raptors will clean up your leftovers. Yes, the cannibalism laws have followed us here too.

Can I get another beer, please??? Oh, I don't care. Surprise me. Yes, a big tip later, oh yeah.

"What... you people are a bunch of pervs." I was merely being polite in today's lingo. Speaking of tipping, please be generous to your waitresses tonight.

You never know, one of them may be bearing my child someday. And they are going to need the money. My children tend to eat.. alot. I'll bet if you give us a cow to eat on Friday, by Monday, nothing but hooves and horns.

We tend to go through a lot of toilet paper also… what… TMI again… damnit."

You see that? Sometimes I talk about awkward things at parties so I don't get invited much anymore. I think the last thing I was invited to one was a Bris… Yeah, that was a good time. Wonderful open bar. Top shelf. Top shelf.

If you're planning a Bris for your child… son… a daughter wouldn't need one… right? Well make sure you have some good hooch in stock. If I have to watch this, I want to get loaded first. And a warm Budweiser just won't cut it. I want to be forgetting it as it is happening.

Do you think this has happened more than once during an Asian circumcision?

The minister starts, "We are here to celebrate the rebirth of little Kyoto Wang's wang..." I'm sorry but that is fuckin funny.

Tipping is important. You have no idea how important. This one waiter I was friends with in New York was a typical dude just paying his bills. If you screwed him on a tip then came back another night and requested him, he'd put a dead cockroach in the bottom of your wife's soup. And he'd watch her eat it. One of those spoonfuls will go crunch, crunch, crunch. And he'll lip read your wife when he says, "What the hell was that?"

And all that might take is just another buck. So go ahead and tip nice, and remember, this is not extortion.

I want to tell you a joke this guy told me the day before he died…

I mean got married. Sorry. The day before, we were making Jack Daniel's investors rich and everyone was telling their favorite joke. So Bob… the groom, stands up and tells this amusing tale…

"A guy's car breaks down in a little town. It gets towed to a garage and the mechanic says, 'This will take all day. Go look at our town.'

So the most popular place to go was "Stan's Sheep Farm." So I'm at the sheep farm and Stan is personally showing my group of nine the best the sheep world has to offer. Everything I never gave a damn to know about sheep, I learned that day. We learned about sheering them and eating them and even breeding them.

As we walk through the pasture and across the meadow, we met Mark Twain. No we didn't. I was just checking something.

So we come to a yard with a bunch of sheep that have big blue ink marks on their backsides. So yes, I'm him. I'm the guy to ask Stan, "Why are there big blue ink marks on those sheep's butts, Stan?"

"Well, we put a big blue ink pad on the male sheep's stomachs. If they have sex with a female, it leaves a blue mark on the females behind."

I'm like, "Did you read that in the 1893 farmer's almanac?" So we're all stumbling around, looking at all the knocked up sheep. All of a sudden, this one sheep appears with a blue mark on its butt... and a blue mark on top of its head. So I bought that little sheep." Silence.

"So I bought that... oh, you guys suck."

So I said, "You know Bob. That story explains a lot." Then we busted out laughing.

He has no respect for comedy as a career choice. So we bust his balls anytime he tells a joke.

And I just gave you the story like it should be told. Bob got lost three times telling it. He'd be like, "So Stan says... wait... Where am I?"

"You're at the freaking sheep farm, dude. Come on, let's get on with it."

That is a long one. Most people can only handle jokes 20 words or less. Like "the farmers crossing the road" joke. No, I'm not giving you the punch line again. I'm not a hack. Or at least my mommy doesn't think so. A quick toast to mothers... "Thank you." Where would we be without mothers? Oh no, I am not going there.

Hey, here's a strange thing you may like to know. The sperm in a man is alive. You can see it under a powerful microscope, swimming around, chasing their tails. The hard part is getting it to stay on the slide without ricocheting off... But I will go there.

Now a female's egg is not alive... otherwise known as... un-living. And our Calvary-like sperm bringing it to life. Looking at it that way, I now consider myself to be more valuable... Nice.

Know what? The last movie I saw, Hangover 2, I was not happy when I left. Did you see it? Half the people liked it, half didn't. I blame the writers on this one. They were probably so burned out from the success of the first one (as they should be), they got three new pages done and stapled it to the front of the first script. "Here dude, another blockbuster." But it's always good to see Tyson.

His scenes in movies are longer than most of his championship fights. 25 years ago, we paid $40 to watch him on Pay Per View. 20 minutes before his fight came on, you peed and got yourself two fresh beers. This was not going to take long. And it didn't. There were times Mike never broke a sweat.

One victim just fell on his ass after a hard right. He actually looked like he was out before he even got hit. Almost like his soul said, "Oh crap." And stepped to the side.

As long as there is no permanent damage and a fat check at the end,

I'd fight Tyson. But I wouldn't want to suffer by being chased and pummeled all night. I'd take a big shot right off the bat. I'd say three things then stick my chin out.

1st- nice tattoo.
2nd- what were you thinking?
3rd- Make my check out to cash.
Good Night.

Mike is probably the nicest guy around but his public image, he's uncaged fury. Why there's not a horror movie called, "Tyson" I'll never know.

Here's the premise baby, sweetheart, baby.

Mike finds out his neighbor made a small fortune putting a bundle on Buster Douglas, who knocked Tyson out.

So Mike shows up at this guy's house dressed as a U.P.S. driver then a meter reader. And whenever the guy opens the door, Mike knocks him out.

Pretty soon the guy stops answering his door. But he does have to venture out. So at Acme, he says to his bagger, "You know, you look like Mike Tyson."

"Whaap." Out again.

At the diner.

"Excuse me waitress? Did anyone ever tell you that you look like Mike Tyson??? Oh crap." "Whaap."

Then Freddy Krueger becomes Tyson and the guy ends up dying with the word "Everlast" imprinted all over his face… If you don't like it then you write a Tyson movie.

And please, have Jack Black be the neighbor. If Jack gets knocked out 20 times in two hours, me and my flask will be there.

Here's another thing. I like talking to strangers. Something will happen and we just start talking. And every once in a while I will be shocked by what somebody tells me. Embezzling… murder. I must have a face people like to confess to. So I'm talking to this sweet old couple in Atlantic City. They were there for their 50th anniversary together.

I said, "That's great. Married 50 years." And the man said, "Were not married to each other. Were married to other people. We've been having an affair for 50 years."

I… was very impressed. Could you imagine keeping a secret like that for 50 years? Amazing. I couldn't live with the guilt. And I'd probably crack on a holiday like Thanksgiving. "Does anybody want a drumstick? I'm fucking another woman… ah crap."

But they were so cute as they blew through their children's inheritance.

You guys like to gamble? I like to gamble sometimes. My first time, I was 18 in Atlantic City with $4 in my pocket. That was about 37% of my net worth at the time. And I turned it into $600 in an hour. And I left. I ran out of there. One of my voices was trying to explain how we can double it.

"I'm not listening. I'm walking." I thought about quitting my job and becoming a gambler. I thought it would always be like this. It's not.

Then I hit that dry spell for about 28 years but I'm back now. And I set my goals lower. Instead of trying to win enough to retire, I'll settle for being left enough to buy a 6-pack.

Most of my gambling consists of the lottery. I'll get two or three big jackpot tickets. And if Elvis wants me to be rich, he'll let me win.

And since we're talking about retiring, I'd like to make a prediction about my retirement.

I'll get that cabin by the lake and within a week, a group of horny, pot smoking kids will show up followed by Jason Voorhees. And you know the horny old cabin owner always gets killed first.

That's the formula. Knock off the adults and leave the children all alone. But you never feel bad for the kids because it's usually the stupid ones that get killed.

"Oh my Elvis, Bobby's dead. Let's jump into the car and go back to the city."

"Ok but I have to get my beer tap out of the cellar and the light bulb just blew out."

Guess who's not coming out of the cellar? They never hear the music. When the scary organ starts playing, go the other way.

That would be great if life was like that. You come to a crossroads in life. You start to turn left and the scary organ starts. So you turn right to the chirping birds and life is good.

But as curious humans, we go left just to try it. See what it's like. It could be anything.

Could be financial ruin or a cockroach in your soup. You don't know. Then how well will you come back from that? Everyone is tough until they have to prove it.

I used to be afraid to go to sleep after a scary movie. I finally thought about it as a movie and after a scene, a director like Woody Allen would yell "cut" and walk over to Jason. "What kind of machete swing was that? I saw my rabbi swing a scalpel at my nephew's Bris with more intensity. I think I saw a pink pen knife over here if that sword is too heavy for you."

Every time I think of Woody Allen, I think of the chain gang scene of "Take the Money and Run."

Like eight guys escape prison chained to each other. They end up at someone's house. And when the homeowner wants to talk to one of them, they all have to use baby steps to move together. Priceless.

A lot of people make fun of Jersey and I don't get it. Except for incredibly high taxes and insurance, it's a great place to live.

We have changes in season.

We have four of them. Did you know that? We have some of the most famous beaches in the world. Even Wildwood has its own catch phrase, "Watch the Tramcar, Please." People come from all over the world to look at our brownish gray ocean. "Are you going in?"

"Hell no. The postcard shows it as blue."

And some of the most famous people ever, have lived in Jersey. Frank Sinatra… yup, he's ours.

Thomas Edison- You might be eating that Jersey tomato in the dark without him.

Even Albert Einstein retired and died here. Smartest man in the world… and he chose to die in Jersey.

And one more little thing. That unpleasantness called "The Civil War"… We were on the winning side. High five, anybody… yeah, there you go man.

I'm telling you, one day, we might just fence ourselves off. We're the "Garden State." We can do this. Right now, we have a sweet deal going. If you want to come in to

Jersey, come on in. it's free. But if you ever want to leave, we charge you at the bridge.

And we keep it all. We even build bridges over land just so you have another toll to pay. We do have a lot of toll roads. When you come into the state, there should be a line of change machines so you can load up on quarters. You're gonna need them.

I'm not saying we're the smartest. We have signs everywhere that say, "Construction will begin on this road on?" They don't know when they can start because they blew all the money on orange barrels and cones.

I know I bust on a lot of things but most of it, I'm just kidding. That's the job. But every president we get, there's always groups of people standing around complaining about the job he's doing. I'd like to follow these assholes to their jobs and yell at them.

Come on, asshole. Flip them burgers, let's go, come on. Don't you hear that buzzer? The fries are done asshole, let's go."

I don't support any politician because I don't believe my interests are at the top of their agenda. You can't do a job well if people are yelling at you. Obama didn't fuck this country up. That was your Bushes and Clintons.

Obama's trying to raise the Titanic and nobody's helping him. Like Bob Dylan sang a century ago, "Don't stand in the doorway. Don't block up the hall." Translation- If you're not helping, then you're hurting.

My final words on politics. As long as I can afford to eat, pay my bills, and my toilet keeps blowing my waste into an alternate universe, I don't give a damn what you do.

Just some simple words from a simple comic in Jersey. Ok- real final words- "I'd rather see Sarah Palin in Playboy then the White House."

Chapter 11
Pets – No, Really

One last thing about Jersey people. We make a pet out of any critter that we can put in a cage. I've known people with pet squirrels, pet groundhogs, even a deer. It would play with you like a dog. Of course, that's in the living room. If you let him out the back door, you'd watch his little white tail just disappear in the distance.

This one guy I know has a scorpion, in an aquarium, on his desk. It's a highly poisonous kinda lobster. You can't touch it… but you can look at it. And it will look at you. And the battle of the wills has begun.

Ben, "I'd like to pet you but you might sting me."

Jake the scorpion, "No, I promise I won't."

Ben, "I don't think he'll sting me."

Jake the scorpion, "I'm gonna sting the shit out of this guy. COME ON SCOOTCH."

When I was about 10, my neighbor had an ant farm. And I learned a lot about ants. Like there are male ants, and all they do is service the queen... squirt squirt.

And when they can't do "the job" anymore, they are given a great meal. Then they are quickly murdered and fed to the upcoming princes for vitality.

See that? Ants are very smart... and cannibalistic. Don't forget to vote.

I always liked snakes but I don't want to own one. I don't want my first thought in the morning to be, "Is Damien wrapped around my throat?" Lots of people get bitten by their pet snakes every year. And they always say, "I didn't think he'd bite me."

He's a snake, dude. That's what he does. For Elvis' sake, read a bible.

I had fish once... I had 10 piranhas. In like, a 200 gallon tank.

They looked like a gang of mobsters, all standing together, looking in the same direction. If one moved to the left, they all moved to the left. One goes to the right, they all follow. I think they were paranoid of each other. If they didn't do exactly what was being done, they might be brunch.

One Saturday, I dropped in a big goldfish for them to eat. As a piranha approached it, another piranha bit the first piranha's tail. He turned around and bit the other one and all of a sudden my piranhas wiped each other out. And I ended up with the most remedial fish in all the oceans.

He just swims around, kissing the water, not even thinking about tomorrow.

And of course, "Charlie" lived to be four years old. Towards the end, he faked us out a few times.

He'd be lying sideways on top of the water. Someone would yell and he'd start swimming around again.

I got my first "adult" pet on my 30th birthday. A friend got me a Siberian husky. Nicest dog in the world. He had two different color eyes. Brown and light blue and that made it hard to win staring contests with him. And just as I was weakening, he'd slap me in the mouth with his tongue. Me and the kids named him "Geronimo" so it stuck. I know, real cute.

Geronimo had a food bowl, a water bowl, and when the kids went over their mothers' house... a beer bowl. He loved that bowl. During football season, we'd go through some beers on Sunday. If anybody got up to get a beer during the game, they had to check Geronimo's bowl.

He lived to the ripe old age of seven. But he really lived. When we'd drive through the drive thru… at a burger joint, you could see the joy in his face. We'd split everything. On Friday nights, we'd split a pizza.

I can't remember if he ever had dog food. But he was probably the happiest dog that ever lived. And it's what he wanted. My sister thought it was cruel. I said, "Well, bring a can of food over and we'll test him." He went for my chili every time.

And I'll bet he died a lot happier than when your dog died. You were probably picking up little Tootsie rolls twice a day all because he didn't know if he was inside or outside. And anytime your dog had to lay down, you had to shove a pad under it, just in case. Yeah, that's just how a dog wants to spend his last two years.

Geronimo drank a bowl of beer, humped a fire hydrant and when he was done, lied down under the shade of a tree and died in his sleep. Where's the Hallmark card for that? That's how I wanna go.

For the moment, I am the guardian of a cat. Cats aren't pets. If you tell your cat that he's your pet, he'll laugh at you. Norton is cool. He's not much of a drinker; he's more of a marijuana buddy.

When I break it out, he'll sit in front of me and wait till I blow smoke at him. After a couple minutes, he'll just stroll over to the Meow Mix bowl and pig out.

I got Norton the old fashion way. I went to a dumpster at a strip mall and hit it a couple times with my crowbar. You get your choice of color and breed leaping out of there. And there was little Norton, nibbling away at an old bagel. I took him home and his attitude was, "Nice house. Now where are you gonna live?"

He got a lot friendlier once he took up pot smoking. Before, he'd only come over to me once one of his bowls was empty. Now he won't leave me alone till he gets high. Then we'll sit around watching Clint Eastwood and Charles Bronson movies all night.

He does try to go out a lot. When you open a door to the outside world, you have to make sure he's not around.

I'll let him out in the winter time when it's two degrees and six inches of snow on the ground. "You wanna go out then go."

He jumps out about five feet then stops. And before I close the door, his little ass is back inside. That's something his little feline mind can't grasp.

One thing about Norton, he hates baths. It's like bathing the Tasmanian devil. I use welding gloves to save my flesh. And when he's done, he'll walk away staring at you. You

Barry Hemmerle

can feel you're being watched... but from where? He can be very unnerving.

A couple times, I actually locked the bedroom door. I could sense his evil.

But I think he's better than most cats. I did toilet train him. Anytime he went for the litter box, I took him to the toilet and gave him a little squeeze. Inside of a week, he was trained. Now my girlfriend bitches to him about leaving the seat up.

Norton is ok. But he did have one bad habit. You know when guys wake up in the morning, laying on your back in bed and you have this blanket tent thing going on down by your groin? Well, Norton liked using this as a scratching post... and that kind of set the tone for the rest of my day.

So last month, I got Norton declawed. He still scratches at it, but now I like it...

Thank you. Thank you so much for coming. See you next time...

ABOUT THE AUTHOR

My name is Barry Hemmerle. I was a bouncer at a comedy club in the mid 1980's. Before Tim Allen broke through, we hung out together and he suggested I take a stab at comedy. After my second show, the manager thought I was good enough to M.C.

Using the name Barry Von, I worked the east coast sharpening my style of sarcastic wit. Besides jokes, I'd occasionally break beer bottles over my head or let audience members rub a spot on my temple for good luck. {It's a bullet someone put there over the beating I gave him as a teen.

My book," The Lost Mind of Buffalo Morgan," is old and new material taken from my shows and woven into a powerhouse of hardcore comedy. There's comedy everywhere in life and this novel will exploit that as fact. From "Let's bolt a cannon to the hood of my car" to "The Good, The Bad and The Ugly of Sex," there's laughs here for everyone.

Is your family insane? It's in here.

Did you celebrate your divorce more than your wedding? UH HUH.

Hate your job? You'll love this book.

I'm giving my fans just what they've been asking for. My next book," Buffalo Morgans, Chronicles from the Asylum," will take you deeper into my comically disturbed mind.....Enjoy!

A SPECIAL THANK YOU TO YOU!

On behalf of everyone at Freedom Of Speech Publishing, thank you for choosing The Lost Mind of Buffalo Morgan: Sick & Funny Comedy from Buffalo's Vegas Show. for your reading enjoyment.

As an added bonus and special thank you, for choosing The Lost Mind of Buffalo Morgan: Sick & Funny Comedy from Buffalo's Vegas Show, you can enjoy discounts and special promotions on other Freedom of Speech Publishing products. Visit www.freedomeofspeech.com/vip to learn more.

We are committed to providing you with the highest level of customer satisfaction possible. If for any reason you have questions or comments, we are delighted to hear from you. Email us at cs@freedomofspeechpublishing.com or visit our website at http://freedomofspeechpublishing.com/contact-us-2/.
If you enjoyed choosing The Lost Mind of Buffalo Morgan: Sick & Funny Comedy from Buffalo's Vegas Show, visit www.freedomofspeechpublishing.com for a list of similar books or upcoming books.

Again, thank you for your patronage. We look forward to providing you more entertainment in the future.

The Lost Mind of Buffalo Morgan
Sick & Funny Comedy from Buffalo's Vegas Show
By Barry Hemmerle

2012 copyright by Freedom of Speech Publishing, Inc.

All rights reserved. No part of this book may be
reproduced, distributed,
or transmitted in any form or by any means, without
permission in
writing from the publisher.

Printed in the United States of America
The publisher offers discounts on this book when
ordered in bulk quantities. For more information,
contact Sales Department, Phone 815-290-9605, Email:
sales@FreedomOfSpeechPublishing.com

Product and company names mentioned herein are the
trademarks or registered trademarks of their respective
owners.

Freedom of Speech Publishing, Leawood KS, 66224
www.FreedomOfSpeechPublishing.com
ISBN: 1938634217
ISBN-13: 978-1-938634-21-5

www.ingramcontent.com/pod-product-compliance
Lightning Source LLC
Chambersburg PA
CBHW071308060426
42444CB00034B/1323